A Do-It-Yourself Approach to Achieving Happiness

Life by Design

Nancy Hunter Denney

To the Robicks family
May you all enjoy each
Ray and in every way
My love
Nancy

Victory, Inc.
Paxton, Massachusetts

To my three greatest passions in life, my husband Thomas, daughter Kaitlin and son Jake. You are the purpose and pleasure in my every day.

Library of Congress Catalog Card Number: 99-76459

Cartoons by Jenny Barton
Cover design by Ana Cordero
Cover Illustration by Lonnie Sue Johnston

Victory, Inc.
581 Pleasant Street
Paxton, Massachusetts 01612
(508) 755-0051

ISBN: 1-930463-00-6

10 9 8 7 6 5 4 3 2 1

Contents

Acknowledgments

This book would not have been written without the inspiration of a few very special people. To this day, they are a constant reminder to me of the power of passion. I wish to acknowledge the following for making a difference in my life, and in the lives of so many others: Dr. T. Mark Morey, Dr. Herb VanShack, Ms. Peg Lowery, the Rev. Will Keim, Marlon Smith, Doug Cureton, Jane C. Root, Mike Jones, Dan Cormany, Sarah Rand, the Rev. Jim Rand, Edith Denney, Dan Witmer, Dr. Marcia Leipman and Dr. Ralph Ianuzzi. My appreciation is also extended to include the memories of Dr. Jerry Saddlemire, Dr. Barry Atkinson and Mr. Marvin, three of the most dedicated teachers I've ever had the honor of knowing.

I wish to thank my editor, Robert Runck, and publisher, Victoria Porras, for taking a chance with me. I also wish to thank author and motivational speaker Marcia Wieder for the dream.

Special thanks are sent to my loving parents. How fortunate to be raised by two people you admire. My continued love to my twin sister, Elizabeth Price, for always being there as a reminder of the power of unconditional positive regard and unyielding acceptance. To my younger and older sisters, thank you for living your lives in a manner that always puts the children first—I have noticed.

The cartoonist, Jenny Barton, is a student leader at a university in Missouri. Her talents are to be enjoyed. I thank her for the time and creativity she gave to this book. I also wish to acknowledge the support of Karen Matt.

I especially want to thank Cindy Elder for her belief in my ideas. It is through her initial words of inspiration and direction that I kept writing and rewriting this book.

Lastly, I wish to thank Jib—the family dog—for her playfulness and need of a daily run.

Introduction

You are standing at your front door—not sure whether to open it or turn around. The only sounds you hear are your own sighs of frustration, aggravation and disappointment. All of a sudden, a voice interrupts your miserable state and asks, "So, what do you want to do?" You don't reply. You can't reply because you don't know what you want to do. You know your life could be better. You know it should be better. But you just stand there in front of the door to your life—stuck.

Maybe you just want to make minor adjustments in your life. Or perhaps you're really churned up inside, and you know that something rather significant needs to change. The size of the change doesn't matter. The important point is that you are willing to do some work on your life . . . starting now.

How to use this book

This book is about the challenges of daily living, the choices you can make and the steps you can take to enter into a life—your life—that is meaningful. You have what it takes to turn your life into a place where you want to spend your time. Written as a do-it-yourself life-improvement manual, Life By Design is a practical guide, complete with how-to tips for organizing, remodeling, renovating, or rebuilding your life.

Inspirational quotes, short stories, and self-reflective exercises are also provided throughout. Working spaces for generating courses of action are provided in the Appendices, where you are free to record your thoughts and work on ideas without interrupting your reading.

How to take your life from where it is today to where you want it to be tomorrow is a practical journey, aided by a variety of tools from your life's toolbox. Enjoy your work.

The Future Is Yours to Create

If you don't know where you're going, any road will take you there.

T his is your life—by design. For as many years as you have been on this planet, you've been working hard. You've built up a considerable amount of "sweat equity" in a particular residential property more commonly known as your life. All of the events that have ever happened in your life are part of this structure. Some events you may have decided to make more important than others; some you might have chosen to exclude. Who you are, at this very moment, is a product of who you have decided to become. You are living the life that you have built.

So, what do you do when you wake up one day to the realization that your efforts have gotten you to a place in which you *don't* want to be, where you feel under-challenged, overwhelmed, or even nothing at all? You may hate the wallpaper and the floors in this house called your life; you might wonder what you were thinking when you picked out that style of furniture (or even who's sitting in it). Your life may now be too complicated, too demanding, or just meaningless. What do you do? The answer is simple: you need a plan.

A plan. It's always good to have a plan when preparing to do something big. Whether you're changing the inside look of your life or building a whole new structure, a plan represents your intention to do something. It is the result of your needs, desires, opinions, and dreams—as you have expressed them. Although you might not always be able to afford what you want to do, you won't know that until you start to put everything down on paper—until you start to create a plan.

When building a house, for instance, a good set of plans—or blueprints—illustrates what the end product (or goal) should look like before any work is even begun. Plans prevent confusion and encourage efficiency and safety. Without such guides, builders work on assumptions, and home-improvement adventurers work on hunches. Plans help determine what needs to happen and when. They guide and direct with the intent of avoiding replication of effort or wasting resources. Plans provide an overview of the work to be done. Here, they represent your dreams, desires and life-improvement goals.

Whether they apply to building your home or your life, the quality of your blueprints depends on your ability to communicate. If you are clear on what you want and don't want in a house, an architect can take your ideas and turn them into a construction plan. But even if you are not sure what you want, an architect can help you figure that out. The architect presents you with suggestions, shows you pictures of houses, and assists you in figuring out what you want versus what you can probably afford—all important functions when building a new home, or even

"I think I understand ... my life is like my house."

Life's journey is just as important as its destination.

a new life. You wouldn't just hand a builder a check and say, "Build me a new house and put it over there." Why, then, would you attempt to create your future without a well-thought-out plan?

The Future Plan is a five-phase guide that uses a life-to-house analogy; it provides the blueprints for your life. Because of that, it makes you the architect by default—or by design. There will be many other areas of specialization that will also be yours to assume, but when you come right down to it, who is better qualified than you are to make and attain your life-improvement goals? You may end up learning a few new skills along the way; you may also end up making a few mistakes. There will be no denying, however, that you are in control of your future, and this fact alone makes the effort worthwhile. You will learn what you need to know as you go along, and you will have many opportunities to keep practicing your new skills and new knowledge as you progress throughout The Future Plan. No one but you can best be trusted with your happiness.

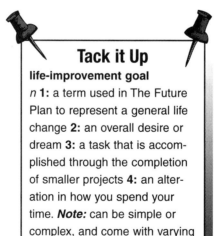

Tack it Up

life-improvement goal

n **1:** a term used in The Future Plan to represent a general life change **2:** an overall desire or dream **3:** a task that is accomplished through the completion of smaller projects **4:** an alteration in how you spend your time. ***Note:*** can be simple or complex, and come with varying degrees of risk.

The Future Plan

Being the architect of your future allows you to see where you are and to decide where you want to go. By following The Future Plan you can select, implement, and evaluate one life-improvement goal at a time, and in a logical fashion. You can channel your energies in a productive and helpful direction. What once may have seemed like an impossible life goal or dream can become quite real. The Future Plan will also assist you in making your intentions clear to others and thereby limit their interference.

The five phases of The Future Plan are similar to steps. Each phase is intended to build upon the one before it, but it may be difficult at times to determine exactly where one phase ends and another begins. You may begin to organize one aspect of your life only to discover that at the same time you want to start fixing up another. In other words, you might start to work on one life-improvement goal (i.e., improving your fitness) only to realize that once this goal is reached, or even before it is reached, you want to start on another goal (i.e., changing your career.)

A life-improvement goal is a significant change you wish to make in your life. Because of this, it requires work. A life-improvement goal is achieved through the completion of many projects, much as a home is built.

Tack it Up

project *n* **1:** a term used in The Future Plan to identify a particular objective **2:** the objective can be simple or complex, small or large, free of risk or with considerable risk **3:** a means to achieving a more general life-improvement goal. *Note:* usually takes more than one project to enhance a person's life and/or to accomplish a life-improvement goal.

How many projects you will need to achieve a life-improvement goal will depend upon the complexity and significance of the goal. For instance, if you wanted to build a new home, you would need to design it, lay out the design on blueprints, dig out and then pour the foundation, do the site work, frame the exterior of the house, and so on. Your home wouldn't be considered finished until work on the interior was completed and the house was in move-in condition. In sum, many projects would be required to build your home—and lots of patience.

Such is the case with your future. It may take many projects—or, sometimes, just a few—to accomplish a life-improvement goal; this is much less tangible than identifying the actions that will be needed to get the job done.

As suggested by the chart that follows, The Future Plan is a guide to help you identify your life-improvement goal(s) by taking the time first to walk around your life and determine how you feel about what you see. The next phase is about where you want to live, followed by the planning, action and evaluation phases. Similar to how I clean my own house, it is possible to breeze through one phase, (i.e., coffee break) yet get hung up in another (i.e., vacuuming)—especially if your life-improvement goal is complicated.

···············The Future Plan

Phase One *Walk Around Your Life*
Observe where you spend your time and how you feel about what you see.

Phase Two *Describe Your Dream Life*
Identify your dreams and passions. Come up with your own definition of "having it all" that feels right to you. Identify your life-improvement goal.

Phase Three *Define the Scope of Your Job*
Draw up the plans for pursuing your dream life, and choose how to proceed.

Phase Four *Begin Your Work*
Put your plans in motion through well-thought-out strategies, actions, and realistic deadlines.

Phase Five *Inspect Your Work*
Take another walk around your life to see what has changed and how you feel about what you've done. Identify other areas of desired life improvement.

> *Unless you try to do something beyond what you've already mastered, you will never grow.*
>
> –Ralph Waldo Emerson

Tools for Your Toolbox

The easy-to-follow format of The Future Plan helps you answer the questions "Where do I start?" and "What do I do next?" The Plan accomplishes this task with self-exploration exercises and numerous opportunities to apprentice new skills and ideas. Self-exploration exercises are designed to be selfish experiences. They will allow you to view your life in many different formats and from many different perspectives. Learning new skills will allow you to continue improving your life.

Self-exploration exercises are invaluable parts of the change process and The Future Plan. The responses come from you and no one else. Think of self-exploration exercises as the tools you need to get the job done. If you've ever tried to hammer a nail using a high-heeled shoe or the handle of a carving knife, then you know what I'm talking about. Tools, like self-exploration exercises, are designed to minimize the amount of effort you have to exert by giving you leverage and precision.

The first tool introduced in this book is a warm-up called "How Do You Know Your Life Needs Changing?" It is relatively simple, not too deep and easy to interpret.

> *Every new project requires a new tool.*
>
> —Thomas Denney

HOW DO YOU KNOW YOUR LIFE NEEDS CHANGING?

Directions: After each statement about your life, circle the response *(TRUE/FALSE)* that feels most accurate.

1. You find yourself living for the weekend. . . . . . TRUE/FALSE

2. Putting the word "just" before you . . . . TRUE/FALSE
describe what you do for a living is a habit.

3. You don't like your friends, but hang out . . . . . TRUE/FALSE
with them anyway.

4. You watch other people exercise on . . . . TRUE/FALSE
television while you sit on your couch
and eat potato chips.

5. You passed up (or will pass up) your ten-year . . TRUE/FALSE
high school reunion because you don't feel you've
done anything worth reporting since high school.

6. When you're asked "What are your dreams?" . . TRUE/FALSE
you realize you've forgotten them.

7. You bore not only your spouse and kids, ... TRUE/FALSE
but your cat has started to avoid you.

8. Nothing you do seems to bring you enjoyment. . TRUE/FALSE

9. Reruns of *Three's Company* crack you up. . . . . TRUE/FALSE

10. You find yourself looking to Jerry Springer . . . . TRUE/FALSE
for advice.

If you laughed, cried, or wondered how I knew all of these things about you, there's no doubt about it—you need to make some changes in your life. It's time to get out of your doorway, take a few steps backward, and place your hand on your chin. It's time for The Future Plan.

The following chart summarizes the fundamental areas of exploration, or the questions that get asked, during each phase of The Future Plan. As you review them, consider whether you already have the answers. If not, a new approach, a different perspective, or a new tool may be needed.

The Future Plan

························· **Phase One**

Walk Around Your Life

Function ➡ To explore the congruency between what matters to you and how you spend your time.

Questions to Ask

What do you see when you look at your life?

What do you hear when you look inside?

How are you spending your time?

························· **Phase Two**

Describe Your Dream Life

Function ➡ To explore your feelings about how your life is going and to determine if change is needed; also, to identify potential life-improvement goals.

Questions to Ask

How do you want to spend your time?

What does "having it all" mean to you?

What are your passions and dreams?

How do you feel about how you are spending your time?

How worthy do you feel of getting what you want?

How do you know it's time to improve your life?

What is your most important life-improvement goal?

••••••••••••••••••••••••••••••••••••• **Phase Three**

Define the Scope of Your Job

Function ⟶ To design the methods for accomplishing your life-improvement goal in a way that is consistent with your comfort level with risk-taking; also, to identify various project ideas.

Questions to Ask

What specific changes (projects) do you want to make in your life?

Which of the four design-build options seem reasonable to you?

What actions will accomplish your life-improvement goal in each of the four risk categories?

•••••••••••••••••••••••••••••••••••• **Phase Four**

Begin Your Work

Function ⟶ To begin the actions necessary to carry out your projects.

Questions to Ask

Are you ready to begin?

What actions on your part will bring about the desired changes in your life?

What plan of personal action is required, in what order, and by when (i.e., in what time frame)?

How do you feel about the progress being made?

How effective is your plan?

Are changes to your plan needed?

How prepared are you to stay within your budget?

.... Phase Five

Inspect Your Work

Function ➡ To recognize your progress and your accomplishments, and to continue to encourage yourself to take control of your future by exploring future life-improvement goals.

Questions to Ask

How does your new life look and feel to you?

What other life-improvement goal—if any—do you want to start now that this life-improvement goal has been achieved?

What new skills have you acquired?

How have you changed personally?

What new perspectives about life have you acquired?

> *Sometimes it's better to have some of the questions than all of the answers.*
> –James Thurber

Hitting The Nail on The Head

\ You deserve to live in your dream life.

\ A plan will help you achieve your dream life by making you the architect of your life.

\ The Future Plan assists you in identifying one significant life-improvement goal at a time and the projects to help you achieve it.

\ The Future Plan has five phases that take you from where you are in life to where you want to be.

\ During each of the five phases, self-exploration questions are asked for you—and only you—to answer.

View from the Curb

Perspective is what results from observing life at a distance.

When you are standing in your front doorway, you can't always see everything in your home. So, too, when your life is being discussed, you can't always hear everything that's being said. Why is that? You're too close. It wasn't until I was able to step back from my own life that I was able to see the disparity between how I was actually spending my time and how I *wanted* to be spending my time. I had to stand out on the curb in order to get a better look at my life. I had to distance myself from all that influenced my perceptions, opinions and decisions.

For instance, consider all of the cultural factors that have the potential to play into your decision-making process (i.e., your ethnic background, education, family, friends, and so on) and then combine them with a host of emotional factors (i.e., your mood, sense of stability, stress level, and so on). Although these factors have gotten you to where you are today—for good or for bad—they don't have to continue directing your choices. However, when you have a clear understanding of their potential role in your past decision making, you are less likely to blame yourself and more likely to keep such factors in their proper perspective when making future decisions.

To explain the premise and inspiration for this book, I have included an excerpt of my life as it once was. My perspective at that time was significantly different from today. I soon realized that I needed to step back—as if I were standing back on a curb looking at the front door of my life—in order to get a better view of what I was doing and why. You will be asked to do the same thing in Phase One of The Future Plan.

By doing this, you will come to realize that life isn't all that complicated. Decisions don't always have to be difficult to make.

Although many factors influence why you live the life you do, two of the most significant factors include your emotional state and your cultural conditioning, which are discussed as they relate to a moment in time—my time.

"From where I stand, my life seems completely under control."

Cultural Conditioning

Born in the 1960s, I am a product of the 1970s and 1980s. Influenced significantly by the political, social, and cultural forces of those times, I grew up believing I could do whatever I wanted and I could be whoever I wanted to be. No longer were my options limited to working full time or having a family; now I could and should do both. Supporting this message was a variety of social changes in politics, the various media, entertainment, literature and education.

For example, during the developmental times in my life, Geraldine Ferraro ran for vice-president, Roe versus Wade was ratified, and Sandra Day O'Connor was appointed to the Supreme Court. The struggle for the ERA Amendment was in full force. Claire Huckstable, a character on television's *The Cosby Show,* managed a full-time law career and motherhood; the Ivy League schools became coeducational, and women's studies emerged as a legitimate field of undergraduate and graduate study. Books like *Sisterhood is Powerful* by Robin Morgan; *Women, Race and Class* by Angela Davis; and *The Feminine Mystique* by Betty Friedan hit the bestseller list. *Cosmopolitan* magazine not only encouraged its female readers to "go for it," but to look sexy while doing so. *MS.* magazine hit the stands, followed by a long line of periodicals that set a new standard for my generation. The future for women was optimistic. From each of these influences, my future direction was shaped.

Emotional Upheaval

Despite all of the positive cultural energy that surrounded me in my twenties, by the time I hit my thirties my life experiences were beginning to contradict my expectations. Specifically, I felt as if there wasn't enough of me to go around. I was a full-time wife, mother and professional. Despite my success, there was a lot of stress in my life and poor coping mechanisms on my part. Trying to keep up with my schedule—see below—was *exhausting*. (Yes, I can hear some of you muttering, "So? What else is new?")

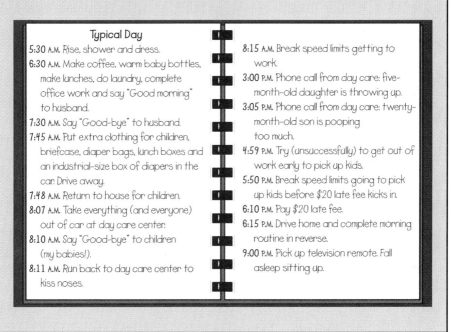

Typical Day

5:30 A.M. Rise, shower and dress.

6:30 A.M. Make coffee, warm baby bottles, make lunches, do laundry, complete office work and say "Good morning" to husband.

7:30 A.M. Say "Good-bye" to husband.

7:45 A.M. Put extra clothing for children, briefcase, diaper bags, lunch boxes and an industrial-size box of diapers in the car. Drive away.

7:48 A.M. Return to house for children.

8:07 A.M. Take everything (and everyone) out of car at day care center.

8:10 A.M. Say "Good-bye" to children (my babies!).

8:11 A.M. Run back to day care center to kiss noses.

8:15 A.M. Break speed limits getting to work.

3:00 P.M. Phone call from day care: five-month-old daughter is throwing up.

3:05 P.M. Phone call from day care: twenty-month-old son is pooping too much.

4:59 P.M. Try (unsuccessfully) to get out of work early to pick up kids.

5:50 P.M. Break speed limits going to pick up kids before $20 late fee kicks in.

6:10 P.M. Pay $20 late fee.

6:15 P.M. Drive home and complete morning routine in reverse.

9:00 P.M. Pick up television remote. Fall asleep sitting up.

What's Your Story?

When you consider the many cultural and emotional factors that influence your desire—and ability—to create a future plan for your life, it's easy to see why change seems difficult. It's understandable that despite good intentions, your life might not be where or what you want it to be. This realization usually only adds to your emotional distress. That's exactly why a plan—The Future Plan—is so necessary.

How do you feel about your life today?
Do you feel in control of your life and time?

The Future Plan was written to give you freedom by offering you choices and helping you to develop your ability to choose. From the interior to the exterior of the structure called your life, from the foundation to the roof, your life can be a reflection of your personal tastes and desires. The Future Plan asks you to think about your dream life and shows you how to make it a reality—your reality. It shouldn't matter what other people see when they stand at your front door or out on your front curb; it matters that you enjoy where you are in your life. It matters that you see a life that brings you happiness.

To give you another way to think about the purpose of The Future Plan, let's go back to our life-to-house analogy. Keep in mind that location isn't always so important. This is an important fact whether you decide to rebuild your life from the ground up or do something less drastic. You've most likely heard just the opposite, however—that "Location, location, location. It's everything!" But The Future Plan is based on the belief that it doesn't matter where you are physically located in your life (your career status, economic status, marital status and the like) as long as you experience a sense of fulfillment, happiness and control over your destiny. I'm reminded of this every time I drive up to the turnpike tollbooth attendant on my way to the airport. As I approach the tiny box with quarters in hand, I wonder why anyone would ever want that job. Then I'm greeted with a sincere greeting and a smile. So, I guess location isn't everything.

How do you think The Future Plan can help you enhance the quality of your life?

> *Stepping back to get a better look at your life can move you forward.*

You can take steps towards greater personal happiness with The Future Plan. When you think of how much time and energy you've already invested in your life, consider how many times you've said, "Build me a new life and put it over there." This is what happens, for instance, when you take a higher paying job with the good intention of providing a better quality of life for your family. But, because your new job requires so much of your time, your family never sees you any more. You have actually degraded your quality of life. Good intentions, bad planning.

This is your life. You are the architect of your future. Before you know it, you will have a set of blueprints worth pursuing—a life by design.

Hitting The Nail on The Head

\ You are a product of whom you've chosen to become.

\ You make decisions based upon your emotions at the time and cultural influences.

\ The Future Plan is a way to enhanced freedom.

Walking Around Your Life

> *Courage is the price that life exacts for granting peace.*
>
> —Amelia Earhart

Have you ever walked into an ice cream parlor looking for your favorite flavor only to be told that they were out of it? The server on the other side of the counter (a good place to be, incidentally) apologizes and informs you that the flavor will be in tomorrow. As you walk out, disappointed, you hear the sound of the bell on the door. Funny, you think, I always used to enjoy the sound of that little bell.

Okay. This is just a minor inconvenience. But why is it that, when we are stressed out, a rather insignificant mishap in our lives makes us think we are doomed? We take a small thing and give it a life of its own. One of the first facts of life we learn as young adults is, "Life isn't fair." Soon afterwards we learn another fact of life: "Bad things happen to good people." Intellectually, we accept this, but not emotionally.

As you prepare to begin Phase One of The Future Plan, "Walk Around Your Life," know that you may be disappointed by what you discover, or you may be delighted. Remember that life has been happening to you since you were born. Some of it has been good and some of it may not have been as good. The important thing is to be honest with yourself. Don't rush the process of self-discovery. Take your time. Contemplate your life. If you don't have an answer to a question, you aren't ready to answer it yet.

In Phase One, you will have to accept what you discover—a realization that requires skill in separating your being from your behaviors. For example, you can be disappointed in your actions, but you can

Low Tide

A couple of summers ago, I took my children with me to a speaking engagement in Newport, Rhode Island. On our way to Newport, we crossed the Jamestown Bridge. Sailboats were scattered on the bay below us—a scene right out of a postcard. But my daughter commented that the ocean looked really yucky. When I asked her why she felt that way, she said, "Because it's low tide. And when it's low tide, you can see all the junk that was covered up before." As we continued on, I thought about what she had said. My five-year-old daughter had found a simple way of making a rather complex point. In life, you often have to experience low tide so that the things you need to work on can become clear. If everything is going well, it's harder to see the areas of needed improvement. Things like success, happiness, job promotions and good health often cover up or compensate for something else that needs to be fixed. High tide makes you forget about the slime and the junk left on the bottom.

still believe you are a good person. Holding onto this belief is what allows you to make it through the downtimes in your life. It is also what will allow you to progress most effectively through Phase One of The Future Plan.

The downtimes—or low tide—are when your life gets totally exposed. Right there lying in the mud is the good with the bad and the junk with the jewels. But what is perceived as a disaster can also become an opportunity. That's why you have to acknowledge what you see and when you see it before it gets covered up again. That's why Phase One of The Future Plan asks, "What do you see when you look at your life?" or "How high or low is the tide in your life?" Remember, if you're not even sure that it's water you're standing in, that's one answer!

The lowest ebb is the turn of the tide.
—Henry Wadsworth Longfellow

Walk Around Your Life

Purpose: *To expose what you see in your life— both the good and the bad.*

Phase One is one of self-discovery through self-exploration. Working within the context of a life-to-house analogy, Phase One begins with a visualization exercise entitled, "My Life Is Like a House." It's your first opportunity to look at your life as if it were your house—to walk around the front yard, look in the windows, go up the stairs and into all of the rooms. Go ahead and stand out on your front curb if you so desire. (I hear this is a good vantage point.)

Phase One begins in your mind with a guided visualization. One of the greatest benefits of such an exercise is its privacy. No one but you can see what you're doing or look into your house. Not only does this give you complete privacy, but you also get permission to be completely honest with yourself. Let your mind be guided by what comes from within you—not by what you think others see or want to see. Open

Tack it Up

visualization *n.* **1:** a term used in The Future Plan to identify a process of self-discovery **2:** a process similar to holding a video camera to your perception of life **3:** a process in which what is viewed depends upon what is asked prior to viewing **4:** a journey into the mind **5:** an activity that can be guided, programmed, or spontaneous.

closet doors in your house, touch the walls, ring the doorbell, and feel the floors under your feet. You can also do the socially unthinkable — you can open the medicine chest and look into the drawers of the side table next to your bed. After all, it's *your* house!

It's All in Your Mind

The goal of your visualization is to help you see the big picture of your life and move on to the details. You will explore the location and setting of your life first, progressing from the general climate and location to the residential property itself, from the exterior to the interior, from the large rooms to the smaller rooms, from under the beds to the tops of the closets.

Remember, visualization takes practice. Be prepared to use more than one take. Practice does make perfect. How warmed up your brain is when you start your visualization will also affect how much you will be able to see. To stimulate your brain requires not only relaxation on your part, but also internal focusing. Keep going until you begin to visualize the details — like holding a video camera up to your eye.

Try to notice things like colors, items, amenities, smaller shapes and so on. It's a take when you are able to describe your mind's walk around your life. Making up what you think you would see — if you had been able to concentrate — is not a take; it's a mis-take. Try again.

One last word of advice before you begin. Don't slam the door and storm out of the visualization if it's not giving you what you want to see. Have fun with it.

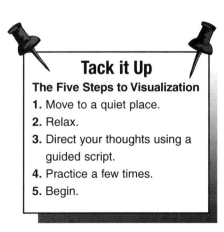

Tack it Up

The Five Steps to Visualization

1. Move to a quiet place.
2. Relax.
3. Direct your thoughts using a guided script.
4. Practice a few times.
5. Begin.

VISUALIZING YOUR LIFE LIKE A HOUSE

Directions: To begin, find a place with only a minimum of distractions. Get into a comfortable and relaxed position. Read the five steps below, then the trigger questions that follow.

1. *Move.* Go to a location with few distractions and little noise. The best locations are those conducive to relaxation and where you won't feel self-conscious.

2. *Relax.* Although best done lying down with your hands at your sides, it's most likely that this isn't an option at the moment because you're sitting in a chair. Loosen any tight or constricting clothing and remove your shoes. (I have found this to be a good technique for clearing a room to gain privacy!) Once you are in a comfortable position, place your hands on your lap with your palms up. Put both feet on the floor. Close your eyes, drop your chin to your chest, lower your shoulders and take five very deep breaths. Inhale and exhale slowly.

3. *Direct.* Review the order of questioning recommended below under the heading, "What to Think About During Your Visualization." It will move your attention from the general to the specific.

4. *Practice.* You are now ready to get relaxed again, close your eyes and imagine yourself stepping out of your car one hundred feet from your front door. Place the "video camera" up to your eye.

5. *Begin.* Give yourself at least twenty minutes to let your mind wander, using the questions below.

What to Think About During Your Visualization

Setting
What is around the structure?
Is it out in the open?
Is it surrounded by lots of other houses?
Is it in a city?
What kind of a view is there?

How close are other things to the structure?
Is there a sense of light or sunshine?
How much space is there?
How much privacy is there?
What is the condition, if any, of the landscaping?

Outside of house

How would you describe the size of your house?
What type of a house is it?
How many floors does it appear to have?
What color is it?
Are there different textures on it?
What is the overall condition of your house?

The way you enter the structure (getting up to and into your house)

How many doors and windows are there?
How do you get into your house?
Are there any paths leading to other entrances?
In what condition are the windows and doors?
What size are they?
Is there a color or texture to them?

Inside of house

How high are the ceilings?
How many rooms are there?
What is the layout?
Is there color?
What kinds of rooms are there?
What is the overall condition of the interior?

Individual rooms

How many windows and doors are there?
What kinds of amenities do you see?
Is there flooring?
How are the walls covered?
Is there color?
What is the overall condition of each room?
What kinds of things are in the rooms?
Is the house neat?

Record It

Don't let your visualization go yet! What you just saw is central to your work in Phase One, Walk Around Your Life. So take a moment now to record your thoughts. Note the size, height, color, texture, condition and overall impression of what you just saw in your mind. Take mental notes on your life. Use the grid below to help you organize your thoughts. You can replicate this graph for interpretation at a later time, or you can use the categories below to organize your thoughts.

MY LIFE IS LIKE A HOUSE DISCLOSURE GRID		
Setting	Individual rooms	House interior
House exterior	House entrance	Overall Impression

Interpreting Your Mind's Footage

What did you see? What does it mean? Your answers are the starting point for Phase One. Interpreting the clips you just produced in your mind isn't too difficult with the use of symbolism. For example, if I had visualized my life years ago, there would have been stuff everywhere, a big heavy door on the front, and the interior would have been a mess. However, the outside landscaping would have been impeccable. Apply symbolism to this, and it reveals that I had too much going on in my life at the time and my plate was too full—hence, the clutter. The difficulty I had opening the big, heavy front door symbolized my fears, insecurities and low self-esteem. The neat appearance on the outside suggested

> *This above all, to thine own self be true, and it
> must follow, as the night the day, thou canst not
> then be false to any man.*
>
> —William Shakespeare

my success at letting others see only what I wanted them to see: the inside mess represented my internal chaos.

Deep, huh? This is the way it is with visualizations. They can be deep or shallow, depending upon how you read the symbolism of the objects and events in your visualization. The process of interpreting these symbols helps you notice things you might otherwise overlook. And how you choose to interpret these symbols is revealing. For example, if you identified lots of windows in your house, to you this might mean that you long for brightness, laughter and freedom in your life. For me, windows represent one more thing that has to be cleaned.

The Right Kind Of Thinking

According to brain-dominance theories, creative thought, imagination, spontaneity, conceptualization and interpretation come more naturally to individuals whose right brain is more dominant than their left brain. The latter prefers specific information and facts presented in a logical manner. If you are right-brained, visualizations come easier to you—and are even fun! Right-brained people tend to be more open to this type of mind exercise.

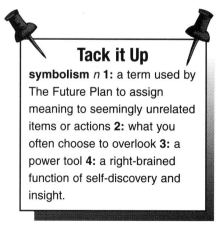

Tack it Up

symbolism *n* **1:** a term used by The Future Plan to assign meaning to seemingly unrelated items or actions **2:** what you often choose to overlook **3:** a power tool **4:** a right-brained function of self-discovery and insight.

> *The greatest deceiver of all is the one that is always with you.*
>
> —Plato

Without a doubt—and regardless of brain dominance—visualizations are subjective experiences influenced by your perceptions and attitude. They aren't as reliable or as valid as standardized methods of assessment, but they are useful in beginning an intimate dialogue with yourself about your life. They are engaging and less threatening than other kinds of self-explorations. Unless you choose to discuss your interpretations and visions with others, only you know what you see.

In this method of self-discovery the hard part is the thinking part. You have to think about how you feel, then decide how you feel about what you think. (To determine quickly which side of the brain you favor, ask yourself if you understood the last sentence. Such a statement is loved by right-brained people and thought to be a waste of time by left-brained people.) Your visualization did produce something. You did see something. To help you make more sense of your visualization, potential symbolic meanings are identified below.

Potential Interpretations for Your Visualization

✓ **Setting (of your house)** = context of your life/location in comparison to others/overall contentment with life

✓ **House exterior** = what others see, appearance, protective layers

✓ **House entrance** = manner in which others enter your life, accessibility, security

✓ **House interior** = real self, relationship of all aspects of your life to each other, internal truths

✓ **Individual rooms** = perceived complexity in your life, degree of comfort versus conflict

Similar video footage can have opposite interpretations. Keep thinking about what *you* think it all means. When you find yourself in a relaxed state, don't be afraid to repeat your visualization to see if it continues to make clear from a distance what you haven't been able to see up close. Visualizations are only as helpful as your ability to learn from what they tell you.

What follows are additional interpretations of what your visualization may have produced. As you read them, ask yourself again, "What else might my visualization be telling me?"

✓ **Setting** = privacy issues, level of responsibility, degree of support, sense of community, quality of existence

✓ **House exterior** = validation issues, perceptions by others, locus of control

✓ **House entrance** = outlook on life, attitude, security issues, vulnerability issues

✓ **House interior** = decision-making control issues, use of time, achievement issues, sense of self-esteem

✓ **Individual rooms** = degree of inner peace, purpose in life, internal condition (peace versus chaos)

As you step back to take a look at your life, consider that your ability to interpret what you have seen is connected to your desire to improve your life and your sense of self-worth. For instance, if you don't feel deserving of a meaningful life, then any life will do. You would be willing to live in any house—even if the roof leaked and the basement flooded. You wouldn't need blueprints or a plan because you wouldn't really care what the results of your efforts created or failed to create. "There. Build my life over there. Build whatever you want." These wouldn't seem like such ridiculous statements if you lacked a feeling of self-worth. There would be no need to focus on how you felt about your life. Why bother?

Well, I think it is important to bother.

Hitting The Nail on The Head

\ Phase One of The Future Plan involves walking around your life.

\ Before deciding how to change your life, ask "What does it look like now?"

\ To see the good, you often have to look at the bad.

\ Visualization exercises allow you to create pictures in your mind that symbolize seemingly unrelated meanings.

My Life as My House

> *How you spend your time is the only true measurement of your priorities in life.*

Walking around your life can reveal many positive things worth celebrating. It can demonstrate the equity you've built up in your life. It can verify that your hard work has brought you many rooms of happiness. The very process of evaluating how you spend your time is the process of evaluating the quality of your life. Phase One allows you to step back and take a subjective and objective look at your life. This requires some effort on your part. It also requires some time.

Your work in Phase One is finished when you have literally drawn a floor plan of your life as if it were a house. You just saw your life in your mind; now the architect in you needs to take over (along with your left brain) and put it down on drafting paper. Your drawing should reflect not what you want your life to look like—or perceive it to look like—but as it actually exists. This will require the use of quantitative units of measure like time and inches, for instance, and an understanding of the term "role."

Tack it Up

role *n* **1:** a term used by The Future Plan that is interchangeable with the word "room," as in a room in a house **2:** a general area of responsibility assumed on a regular basis, such as parent, wife, domestic engineer, student, church member **3:** the ordinary behaviors of being human, such as sleeping, eating, watching television.

In preparation for your drawing, think about what you do with your time—what roles you assume. In a house, you would usually find a bathroom or two, a few bedrooms, a kitchen, a living room and so on. In your life, you would also find a few standard roles, such as sleeping, working or being a parent. To help you organize your thoughts, you will be invited shortly to complete the "As Time Goes By" chart found in Appendix A (in the back of the book).

You can be as specific or as general as you'd like to be about your roles in life, but as a guide, your list of roles should represent the more significant roles you assume—the major headings under which smaller tasks fall. Below is a sample chart taken from my life.

As Time Goes By

Role	Examples of Filling Role	Hrs. Per Week
Professional educator	researching topics, traveling, giving workshops	30
Being human	sleeping, watching television, eating	60
Domestic engineer	performing housework, grocery shopping, doing laundry, cooking	20
Community volunteer	serving as a classroom parent volunteer	5
Mother	playing with the kids, taking the kids places, helping with homework	40
Wife	spending time alone with spouse talking, going out to dinner	13
	Total per week	168 hours

Roles become your life's rooms. If a week only has 168 hours in it, and you spend sixty hours a week at work, that leaves you with 108 hours. If you sleep eight hours a night, that leaves you with fifty-two hours in your week to divide up among other roles you list. The largest room in your house, therefore, would have to be labeled "work." Remember, quality—not quantity—is what counts. You don't get points for having the most roles (only the most toys).

Below is a sample drawing of "My Life Now as a House" which illustrates how you will use the information from your "As Time Goes By" chart to draw your life as a house in Appendix A. Each square of the graph paper equals one hour of time. So, a total of 168 squares needs to be filled. If your house has more squares filled, then you've just given yourself more than twenty-four hours a day, or more than seven days in a week. Good try. To complete Phase One of The Future Plan, go to Appendix A now.

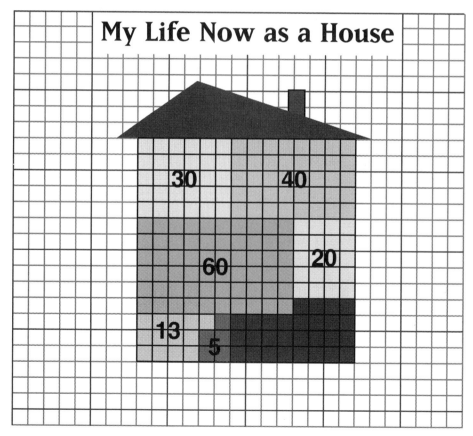

Who controls how you spend your time and its quality?

What is potentially covering up your ability to see your life clearly?

The questions that follow are designed to help bring meaning to your drawing. This is an important summary step in Phase One that allows your right brain and your left brain to interface for awhile.

- How do you feel about the number of rooms in your house?
- Which room in your life seems the smallest?
- How do you feel about that?
- Who or what determines which rooms are in your house?
- Which room(s) appear to be missing from your house?
- In which room(s) do you like to spend most of your time?
- Which room(s) do you wish you could redecorate or demolish?
- What does your floor plan tell you about your life?
- What would you have to do to make this house your dream house?

Simple Addition

Five months after my daughter was born, I gave an evening leadership workshop on a college campus. About twenty student leaders were in attendance. During the program I spoke of my children, as I often did. At the end of the program, a student asked me, "How many hours a day are your children in day care?"

My first response was, "Not many. Only when I'm at work." Since this particular student was a left-brained engineering type, he asked, "How many hours is that?" I sighed, turned to the chalkboard, did the math, and responded, "Ten." (Yes, I needed the board to do that; the student was surprised, too.) "So," the student continued, "Your children spend fifty hours a week, on average, in child care."

I had chosen to believe, until that student questioned me, that I spent more time with my kids than I did. What about you, and how you spend your time? Does your life as a house look the way you want it to? Do the comparative proportions, as in my enlightenment, suggest a different truth?

Ignorance may be bliss, but it doesn't move you forward.

Time Doesn't Lie

Using time as your guide, it becomes harder to make subjective guesstimates of room sizes because either you spend a majority of your time being in (and doing) the role of employee, for instance, or you don't. You either spend thirty hours per week cleaning your house, doing the shopping and taking care of other domestic activities, or you don't. (In my case, I don't.) Therefore, it is the quality, as well as the quantity, of your time that influences how you feel about your life.

I learned that quality time is only half of the equation. I also learned that who controls the quality and quantity of your time is important. You should always be in control of your time. It's yours. Only you can direct how it is used. But you have to believe that. You also have to believe what the numbers are telling you.

Wallpaper and Other Cover-ups

The process of stepping back to look at your life and how you spend your time is like wallpapering. Sometimes there's a risk in stripping off wallpaper because you don't know what you'll find underneath—just like when you step back and look at your life. Often, nothing was wrong with the layers underneath; they just went out of style. New patterns covered the old patterns.

If you've ever wallpapered, then you know that there are two important rules that can't be broken or your project may not come out as planned. The first rule is that you never, under any circumstances, wallpaper with your significant other. The second rule is that when you break rule number one, you have no one to blame but yourself. Trust me—nothing good can ever come from two emotionally connected individuals attempting to line up edges, get rid of bubbles, stop free-flowing goo from dripping all over a new rug, or make a pattern match. A pattern, incidentally, that one loves and the other hates.

Whether you want to accept it or not, what is under the layers of wallpaper continues to influence your life—often for the good. You don't have to live in the past, but what's under the layers does have the potential to be exquisite, and to provide a beautiful source of enhanced understanding.

There comes a time during Phase One work when you do have to accept where you live so you can build upon it, start over, renovate, or tidy things up a bit. Struggles for truth take time, as does acceptance of the truth. In my experience, Phase One and Phase Two are the longest phases to work through for these reasons. Give yourself time to contemplate the ideas being presented in each phase and apply these ideas to specific areas of your life that need some work—or to your entire residence, if needed. It took you years to build the equity in your life; it may take some time to capitalize upon it.

Deciding what's really important in life can take a lifetime. The goal of The Future Plan is to bring home the realization that time is passing. Your life is passing. *Now* is when you need to start making decisions about self-improvement, enhanced happiness and greater self-actualization. The size of the change isn't important. Where you live isn't important. Believing in the power of making choices is what moves you ahead and keeps you alive.

Hitting The Nail on The Head

   \ How you spend your time reveals your true priorities in life.

   \ Who controls how you spend your time affects the quality of your life.

   \ Wallpaper is a great way to cover up what you don't want to see or choose to ignore.

   \ Never wallpaper with someone you love.

   \ The truth can set you free.

Describing Your Dream Life

> *All our dreams can come true—if we have the*
> *courage to pursue them.*
>
> —Walt Disney

I magine waking up every day to the realization that you are living in your dream house. You look around and love what you see, from the window treatments to the size of the closets. Your Jacuzzi is almost too big. The walls are the perfect color, and the windows provide a view of the beautifully landscaped yard—just like the ones you've admired in magazines. As you go out to the hallway, you smell the coffee already brewing. Life is good.

As you pour your coffee, you notice the mug you've chosen. It's one of those inspirational mugs often exchanged at holiday office parties. The saying reads, "I'm contemplating life. It only looks like I'm sleeping." You chuckle, then walk back to your bedroom as you take another sip of coffee. You sit at the end of your bed, and realize that life doesn't get any better than this. You live in your dream house and the mortgage is paid off. You feel alive.

But then—abruptly—your dream ends. You open your eyes to the familiar sound of your alarm clock. Life goes on.

The ironic thing about dreaming is that your mind lets you pretend that what you experience in your dream is your reality. You even experience emotions while you dream—often so strong that your body responds. Have you ever sat straight up in bed, heart pounding, mind racing, because your dream seemed so real? If the answer is, "Of course," then you know what it's like to have your subconscious at work while you are at rest (asleep).

Likewise, have you ever been sitting somewhere, surrounded by people, fully aware of your surroundings, yet so deep in thought (daydreaming) that your mind is a thousand miles away? It's like taking a vacation without having to pack. You just go. Daydreaming is when you let your mind take the rest of you to a place you'd rather be—or to a place that has been on your mind, yet hidden. If you don't particularly like what you are seeing while daydreaming, you simply tell your mind to drift somewhere else. You are in control of these daytime dreams.

Describe Your Dream Life

Purpose: *To explore what would bring contentment to your life through the pursuit of your passions and priorities in life, and to ultimately identify one life-improvement goal.*

The second phase of The Future Plan, "Describe Your Dream Life," urges you to believe in the power of your mind to direct your thoughts, just as it would in daydreaming. You have the ability to focus, revise and redirect where your mind is going. You can add your desires, goals and aspirations to the journey so the destination is one of your choosing, not one chosen for you. You have successfully passed through Phase Two when you can articulate one significant life-improvement goal to take on. You are able not only to tell yourself this is your goal, but you are also able to tell others.

Many external and internal factors affect your ability to do and say what you want in life. The most significant of these factors is how worthy you feel of living your dream life and how prepared you are to start working towards it. It may be necessary in Phase Two to start considering how proficient you are at living life. Do you have all of the skills you need? The tools at your disposal throughout The Future Plan won't be of any value if you don't know how and when to use them.

> *Either this man is dead or my watch has stopped.*
> —Groucho Marx

You might be surprised (or impressed) by what you already know about how to live a meaningful life and by your ability to apply this knowledge to your everyday life. It only makes sense that the more you apply what you know, the more you control your destiny.

In order for The Future Plan to be useful in your search for a more meaningful life, there needs to be some agreement on what is meant by "meaningful," just as there needs to be agreement on what is meant by "dream life." Both terms are used interchangeably with "contentment." The Future Plan is based on the premise that only you can define contentment. If becoming rich (or richer) is how you define contentment, than that's what it means to you. However, if you feel that being at the bottom of the food chain is all you deserve, then there's work to be done!

"Is that your final offer?"

> *There is only one success—to be able to spend your life in your own way.*
>
> —Christopher Morley

Being content is about finding a balance in your life. It's about being satisfied with the quality of your life so that you fall asleep at night thinking, "I'm truly happy. I have a great life." This understanding celebrates life—the moments to the months. It slows down the clock and asks that you stop long enough to find the meaning *in* your life, not the meaning *of* your life.

Being content is a nice thing to be. But some of the most successful and richest people aren't content with their lives. They never seem to have enough or to be enough. They can't move fast enough, climb high enough or make enough—because they haven't stopped to ask, "What is enough?" They haven't contemplated contentment.

Although you may be socialized to believe that there's got to be more to life than simply being content, keep in mind that being content does not mean to be without thrills, adventure and risk; in fact, it's just the opposite, for it is often during the pursuit of these things that you find contentment.

Knowing what is most important to you and what has little significance helps you to determine how you spend your time and why you spend your time that way. You are in a position to define true happiness when you are clear about what really matters: your priorities. A meaningful life is achieved when the way you are spending your time reflects *how* you want to be spending your time. This is when you know you own your life and are not leasing or renting it.

How can you organize your daily living in a manner consistent with your priorities in life?

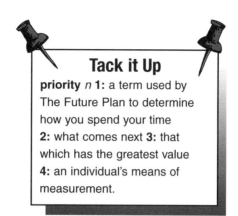

Tack it Up

priority *n* **1:** a term used by The Future Plan to determine how you spend your time **2:** what comes next **3:** that which has the greatest value **4:** an individual's means of measurement.

Place great hope in the value of moments. Try to believe that the moments become the minutes, the minutes become the hours, and the hours become the days. Phase Two wants you to explore how you feel about time, with the hope that you will come to appreciate its limitations while acknowledging that there are no guarantees. If you don't make the connection between time and priorities, then you allow nature to create your future—whenever it gets to it—or if it even gets to it at all.

How you are passing your time is how you are passing your life. Do you wake up in the morning with the belief that there is a reason for getting out of bed? Do you rush to your closet and ask, "What am I going to wear to celebrate my life today?" or do you ask, "What do I have to wear to my dull job today?" (I usually ask, "What's clean in here?")

But whatever your reason, whatever your priorities in life, it's important that your decisions are consistent with them—that *your* behaviors reflect *your* priorities. Whether it's putting your kids on the school bus in the morning, putting on a new tie, or putting the pillow behind your head so you can finish reading a great novel, the important thing is that you derive pleasure from doing whatever you do. Lots of little things or the pursuit of one big thing can give your life meaning.

Every second of every day doesn't have to be like a trip to Disneyland—which can be greatly overrated if you are toting around two young children in one-hundred-degree weather and the only water at your disposal costs what you paid in airfare. But your life should have purpose—a reason to get up every day. There needs to be something that powers your mind, body and soul. That something has a name. It's called passion.

One of the reasons so many people don't follow their dreams is that they don't understand what it means to have passion. Passion is about all of the possibilities, not just the ultimate dream. Much like having it all can only be defined by the person who will or will not have it all, passion can only be defined by the individual whose life will be empowered by it. The characteristics and feelings associated with this internal sense of will are difficult to describe because passion is so personal.

Life is about growing and changing as a human being. It's about waking up to your dream life with a hot cup of coffee waiting for you in a mug with your name on it. When you can imagine a better life, a different you—in your dreams, as well as while wide-awake—you can make it happen. Maybe you don't have all of the skills or understanding you need at this very moment to be the architect of your future, but you do have a plan—The Future Plan. The only thing that can prevent you from achieving a more meaningful life is you.

Hitting The Nail on The Head

\ Phase Two involves describing your dream life.

\ You often have to develop your personal skills in order to define your dream life.

\ Contentment in life is a goal worth pursuing.

\ The minutes in life become the days, weeks and months.

\ To dream is to imagine the possibilities of life.

\ Coffee mugs don't even need to have coffee in them to brighten your day—but it helps.

Power Tools and Passion

> *Begin at once to live, and count each day as a separate life.*
>
> —Seneca

To discover how important passion is in life, look at how some people pursue the game of golf. Maybe you are a golfer and understand this passion (or you're married to a golfer, so you pretend that you do). You subscribe to every golf magazine published. The soaps in your bathroom are in the shape of golf balls. Your golf bag is a permanent fixture in the trunk of your car, just in case your car breaks down near a driving range. You would play golf in a snowstorm, and you dream of wearing the Green Jacket some day. Your passion for golf is not an all-or-nothing proposition, because you have made it a big part of your daily life. This pursuit—directly or indirectly—brings you joy and contentment, even if you never win the club championship.

You don't always have to use your passion to know it's there. Look at passion as if it were a current of electricity flowing through your being. It flows continuously, whether it's needed or not. You know it's there, and you're paying for it monthly! The price of passion is quickly disregarded when the need to use it is high enough.

Are there ever days when everything that needs electricity is not only plugged in, but also turned on? For example, your dishwasher is running, your oven is baking, your tape deck is playing and you're checking your e-mail on the computer. At the same time, your vacuum is running, your dryer is spinning and you've got hot water filling your bathtub. There are also days when everything is plugged in, turned on and the meter is running—but you're not even there!

Tack it Up

passion *n* **1:** a term used by The Future Plan to represent the ultimate power source **2:** an internal motivator **3:** what you feel from the inside out **4:** possibilities.

What would happen if you never wasted this internal energy source, but tapped it nonstop? Like most people, you can't always afford to channel all of your energy—at once—into the pursuit of your passions. Although this is an option, this would be a narrow way of defining what it means to have passion.

You should incorporate passion into your existing life as you see fit—without blowing a fuse. Too much too quickly isn't always the best use of your energy. For example, if you've ever decided to get back into shape by running five miles a day (and you've never run a single mile before in your life), after the first couple of days running this distance, you stop. You ache. Despite the pain relievers and hot baths, you're not internally inspired to put on your sneakers. You can't make yourself do it. That's because you literally blew a fuse! There was too great a change, made too quickly, to your normal routine. Putting too much passion—or power—into achieving your goals is like using a nail gun to hang a picture on the wall. Although I've seen it done, it's overkill.

> *Poor is the man whose pleasures depend on the permission of another.*
>
> —Madonna

Power tools can be exciting. If you've ever used a nail gun, you know what I mean. This tool can shoot nails into wood as fast as you can pull the trigger. This is significantly faster than the rate that the average handyperson can swing a hammer and strike a nail on the head. Once you've used a nail gun, it's hard to turn back. They are faster, easier, make a pleasing popping sound and can make you feel like Rambo.

A compressor is needed to operate a nail gun, but that just adds to the thrill of it. A compressor is another tool that requires electricity—and earplugs. In combination, these two inventions give new meaning to life. To say that my handyman husband loves his nail gun would be an understatement. I only get concerned when he wears his nail gun in a holster and walks around the house saying, "Hasta La Vista, Baby."

In Pursuit of Passion

Passion comes from within; therefore, it isn't visible to those around you—unless you choose to make it visible. It may not even be visible to you at this point.

There are many ways to get in touch with your passions. Believe that the current is running, even if you don't have anything plugged in at the moment. The light is on. You are home. Think about those activities, places, people, things and so on that qualify as passions for you. Jot them down on the "Passions Inventory" found on the next page.

The Power Of Words

Power tools don't work if you don't plug them in. To pursue a passionate life means to seek outlets actively. Your perceived quality of life determines how many outlets you have at your disposal on any given day. On good days, you may have an outlet for whatever needs to get charged up, inspired or maintained. On bad days, your outlets may be jammed by other sources of energy-zappers (your baby-sitter cancels at the last minute, a deadline gets pushed to an earlier date, thunderstorms cut short your golf game, your child throws lunch across the room). Any effort to expand the capacity of your overloaded outlets fails; you are literally tapped out.

PASSION INVENTORY

Directions: What are your passions? Are they being pursued?

	Yes	No
1.		
2.		
3.		
4.		
5.		
6.		
7.		
8.		
9.		
10.		
11.		
12.		
13.		
14.		
15.		
16.		
17.		

There may be outlets at your disposal, yet you are unaware that you've put a coffee table, chair and bookcase in front of them. Your efforts to enhance one room in your life may be blocking or preventing additional sources of power from becoming known to you. On the next page is an exercise called "Word Power," intended to help you get a clear picture of how you perceive the role of passion in your life. Because passion can be found (and disguised) in many ways, "word associations" are used to help you describe your life.

 How do you perceive your ability to pursue your passions in life?

Remember, passion can show itself in many ways. It can appear in your dreams, hobbies or—as we get older—in what we want to do after we retire. But life is meant to be lived now, not later. Every second that passes is a second of your life that you don't get back.

The pursuit of your passions is both ongoing and ever changing. What excites you today may not bring you any pleasure tomorrow. That's why it's so important to stay in touch with your passions as you mature, experience life and change your priorities in life. Knowing your passions will help you identify possible life-improvement goals and draw your dream life.

 What brings you pleasure?

You have passion. The hard part is liking yourself enough to believe that you are allowed to plug stuff into it. You may stand around holding happiness in your hand and regret (or resent) that you can't turn it on because it requires an expenditure of energy on your part. The only one who can prevent you from letting passion guide your life is you. Let what brings you inner joy guide your choices. Make the pursuit of your passion part of everyday life.

WORD POWER

Directions: Circle the word in each row that best characterizes your life.

hammer	nail
free	trapped
child	adult
young	old
alive	dead
emotion-filled	empty
curious	rational
happy	sad
hopeful	hopeless
spirited	stalled
spontaneous	programmed
excited	bored
yearning	existing
full	empty
healthy	unhealthy
laughter	tears
energized	drained
flexible	rigid
valued	worthless

Any words circled in the left-hand column characterize feelings of passion and contentment, while right-hand column words are typically associated with a lack of passion or feelings of uneasiness. What you have identified from this list is a beginning, not an ending.

Tack it Up

limiting beliefs *n* **1:** a term used in The Future Plan to represent a block **2:** self-created negative statements or beliefs, employed consciously or subconsciously, and used to protect you from failure.

Don't Pull The Plug

One way to pursue your passions is to eliminate what's holding you back. Such things are called "limiting beliefs." Although they may seem harmless, such self-created statements damper your creativity before you even begin to draw your dream life on paper. They disrupt your forward movement. But limiting beliefs are really just excuses. They are employed consciously and subconsciously by you to protect you from failure. The true failure is listening to them.

Because they are negative, limiting beliefs disconnect your passion from the possibilities of your future. Limiting beliefs are clever. They let you discover what other people think about your pursuits without risking their judgment. How can you be blamed for something you claim not to have done?

Before completing the work of Phase Three, you will need to identify and free yourself from limiting beliefs. You will need to think more positively about the possibilities in life. Focus on positive self-talk. Let go of words and phrases that stop your dreams from becoming your reality. Give yourself permission to be happy.

Limiting beliefs disconnect your passion before your life gets turned on.

Limiting beliefs start with such phrases as:

- 🖎 If I had all the time in the world…
- 🖎 When my kids are finally out of the house…
- 🖎 Maybe after my husband retires…
- 🖎 If it weren't for our health insurance coverage…
- 🖎 In reality what will happen is…
- 🖎 Only after I win the lottery…
- 🖎 Only after my parents win the lottery…
- 🖎 It will never happen, but…
- 🖎 I know you/they won't let me, but…

Give yourself permission to move if you don't like where you live. Allow yourself the pleasure of spending more time with your children—if that's what you want. Free yourself from time-consuming activities—if that's what you want. Accept that you love your hobby and hate your job, so find a way of making your hobby pay the bills—if that's what you want.

You are worth so much more than just the roof over your head. The walls in your dream life should be the color that brings you pleasure. The windows should bring in sunshine, brightness and light—if that's what you like. The rooms should be just the size to make you feel comfortable and furnished in a manner that reflects your style and taste. Go ahead and pursue your passions! To explore what they might be in more detail, take the "Passion Pursuit" exercise on the next two pages.

PASSION PURSUIT

Directions: Take a few moments to complete each sentence below as honestly as possible. You may discover a few passions along the way.

My favorite hobby is

_____

The person I most admire is

_____

I admire this person because

_____

When I (we) retire I'm going to

_____

The greatest gift I have is my ability to

_____

The three places on earth that are like heaven to me are

_____

I have always dreamed of living in

_____

If/when I am ready to commit to someone, it will be because he/she is

_____

If I had known a year ago that the world would end tomorrow, I would have

_____

When my children think of me, I want them to think

_____

I am happiest when I

_____

If I were given three magazine subscriptions, I'd want

_____

I laugh most often when

_____

When I think of fun, I think of

_____

The trait I admire most in others is

_____

If my friends were to write my obituary, it would read

_____

It would be a blast to

_____

If money weren't an issue, I'd become a/an

_____

To be totally free means

_____

In moments of silence, I think of

_____

The one thing I love doing more than anything else is

_____

Passion brings purpose to your life.

Your life was meant to be lived with passion. You may not always score a hole in one, but the very act of putting on your golf shoes, walking the greens, swinging the club and being outdoors is worth the effort. Daily contentment resulting from the pursuit of your passions is like scoring a hole in one.

Ways to Plug in Your Passion!

- Read motivational books.
- Start attending religious services on a regular basis.
- Pursue a friendship with someone you admire.
- Improve your fitness.
- Hang out with your children or baby-sit others' children.
- Spend ten minutes each morning in complete solitude.
- Turn off the television for two months.
- Stand in the middle of a bookstore and go wherever your curiosity sends you.
- Start a daily journal.
- Listen to motivational tapes on your way to work.
- Talk about your inner desires with people you trust.

Hitting The Nail On The Head

\ Passion is the ultimate energy source.

\ Life is meant to be lived with passion.

\ Passion is a personal thing defined only by you.

\ A power tool is a lot like a passion. Neither one works if it's not plugged in.

\ Passions can appear in many different forms.

\ You have to play the game of golf if you ever expect to score a hole in one.

The Self-Worth Builder

I buy women's shoes, and then I use them to walk away from me.

—Mickey Rooney

Have you ever found a baby-sitter, carpenter or house cleaner who was so competent that you didn't tell anyone else about them—not even your closest friends? You kept this information to yourself for fear that if you did recommend any of these people, you might not be able to get hold of them when you needed them. So you said nothing. Your sense of possessiveness dominated your sense of fairness. Even when you were asked, "Do you know anyone who is good at doing home improvements?" you did what most people do in similar situations—you lied.

When provoked to tell a lie, I am more likely to break out into laughter than actually be dishonest. This is not to say, however, that I haven't found myself in a dilemma every now and again over disclosing terrific resources. It's my standard mode of operation to change the subject quickly when asked to reveal such delicate information. Persistent friends, however, are not fooled by my attempt at diversion. Eventually, I crack under the pressure.

Does this situation sound familiar to you? Can you recall times when you've ended up being a victim of your own kindness? You may have shared information when you could have been more creative (misremember the phone number of a valuable resource). As a result, you may have had to look for another competent service provider—or been willing to wait until the resource you gave away could fit you in.

Tack it Up

self-worth *n* **1:** a term used by The Future Plan to represent the value you place on yourself **2:** an estimate or opinion of oneself; **3:** a concept comprised of your self-esteem, identity and self-respect **4:** basis from which personal change is made.

Reliance on yourself—and only yourself—to make your life a better place in which to live is the most economical and prudent course of action. You have what you need, when you need it, and if you don't, you know what you need to learn or do to get what you need. There's no need to lie or deceive your friends, because you are your own most valuable resource.

This newfound honesty is freeing in many ways. After all, deception doesn't move you forward. Learning new ways of identifying what will make your life more meaningful (or content) moves you forward. How you proceed from this point on will depend upon how honest you can be with yourself.

Do you like you?

Placing a Value on Yourself

Only you can determine what true happiness is worth to you. This value is directly proportional to the value you place on yourself, which is called your self-worth. A healthy level of self-worth is essential for making life changes because it makes you feel that your efforts are worthwhile. You are worth the risk and the outcome—good or bad. A high degree of self-worth means you care enough about yourself to spend resources on your life—resources that include your time, money and talents. Cost becomes relative. Your happiness becomes the priority. The self-worth builder learns not only why a positive personal perspective is so important to The Future Plan, but how to go about building upon what is already there—a life-long skill.

> *Life is the most precious gift we are ever given, the true value of which is measured by our self-worth.*

Without a high level of self-worth, you have no motivation to change because you don't feel worthy of a better existence. You also aren't willing to take the time and energy to plan for change. Everything you read becomes useless information until you feel deserving enough to put it into practice in your life, for your benefit.

A positive personal perspective (which is interchangeable with the term "high self-worth") is characterized by the acceptance of your rights as a human being to be respected, to teach others how you want to be treated, to dignity, and to the right to love and be loved. You also have the right to own your own life and the right to change your mind. When you have a high degree of self-worth, these rights guide your efforts. You think and act accordingly. As a result of being your own self-worth builder, your dream life/dream house blueprints will more accurately reflect your true desires. You will begin to feel worthy of standing up for what you want.

The Inner Triangle

I am frequently asked how to build self-worth. Although this process doesn't happen overnight, simple changes in how you look at yourself can bring about significant changes in how you act and think. I've taken a rather complicated topic and broken it down into a few circles and a triangle; I call these ideas The Inner Triangle. It is based on the belief that inside all of us is a triangle containing three constantly growing or shrinking inner circles, labeled "self-esteem," "self-identity," and "self-respect."

Inner Triangle of Self-Worth

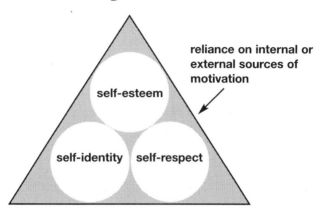

Definition of Terms

Self-worth incorporates all three of the following concepts and suggests that they are linked to one another.

Self-esteem is how you feel about yourself. It focuses on your feelings of self-love or self-hate and helps you to answer the question, "Do I like me?"

Self-identity is your definition of self: how you describe your personality, appearance, skills, traits, and so on.

Self-respect celebrates the value you place on yourself in relation to other people; it is reflected in how you handle your interactions with others.

External motivators are perceived or real beliefs about how you should act or think. They come from someone else or from something not under your control.

Internal motivators are things from within you that influence and drive your behavior.

The size of your inner triangle determines whether or not you rely on internal or external motivation as your source of inspiration. A small inner triangle indicates a reliance on external motivators. A large inner triangle indicates significant reliance on internal motivators. Although others may give you advice, you ultimately make your own decisions

Tack it Up

Examples of Motivators

External	Internal
• parental approval	• love
• peer pressure	• beliefs
• food	• a sense of purpose
• money	• goals
• job promotions	• passion
• school grades	• a sense of responsibility
• group acceptance	• faith
• membership	• priorities
• fame	• a positive outlook on life
• praise	• personal ethics
• external recognition	• aspirations
• socioeconomic status	• a sense of right and wrong
• the opinions of others	• desires
• the expectations of others	• spirituality
	• a desire to make a difference
	• relationships/friendships

and form your own opinions consistent with your morals, values, aspirations and other attitudes. It is through the use of internal motivators that you ultimately change and move forward.

Your goal is to have a large inner triangle. By increasing your reliance on internal motivators and decreasing your reliance on external motivators, you can build your self-worth. Focus on behaviors and attitude changes that center on and are consistent with your goals, aspirations and sense of purpose. There are practical ways of doing such things once you get a sense of how much you like (or don't like) yourself.

One way to do this is to complete the Circle of Self-Inventory found on the next page. This self-exploration exercise requires more than your mental notebook; you will need a pen or pencil because the answers need to be grouped as part of the interpretation process. Are you ready?

CIRCLE OF SELF-INVENTORY

Directions: Place a check mark next to the choice that best fits your personal perspective.

1. I continually work on improving myself.
2. I haven't done anything to grow lately.
3. I have a strong desire for knowledge.
4. I achieve my goals.
5. I maintain dependent relationships.
6. I have a tendency to cheat or lie about the small stuff.
7. I am an effective communicator.
8. I take care of myself.
9. I control my own destiny.
10. I have a negative outlook on life.
11. I seek direction from others about my life, and I do what I'm told.
12. I take care of my appearance.
13. I have poor health habits.
14. I drink too much.
15. I make a difference.
16. I feel sorry for myself.
17. I respect myself.
18. I consider myself an ethical person.
19. I have no goals.
20. I don't engage in high-risk behaviors such as smoking, or I am trying to quit.
21. I demand that others respect me.
22. I let others control me.
23. I maintain healthy relationships that are mutually beneficial and rewarding.
24. I maintain relationships with people I really don't like.
25. I don't lie.
26. I have a positive outlook on life.
27. I resist change.
28. I ask for advice, not answers.
29. I have let my appearance go.
30. I am open to change.

31. I only seek more knowledge as a means to an end.
32. I maintain a strong support network of friends, colleagues, etc.
33. I know I don't communicate well, but I don't do much about it.
34. I have an annual health checkup.
35. I like who I see in the mirror each morning.
36. I am not happy with who I am.
37. I know how to ask to be treated with respect by others, or I am working on it.
38. I only go to the doctor when I'm very sick.
39. I often feel as though people walk all over me.
40. I put the needs of others ahead of my own on a regular basis.

Scoring. Now go back through your answers. Circle the following numbers: 1, 3, 4, 7, 8, 9, 12, 15, 17, 18, 20, 23, 25, 26, 28, 30, 32, 34, 35, 37. Count how many of the statements for the circled numbers you checked off; write the total on the line below.

Total _____ = Circle Of Self-Inventory Score

Circle of Self-Inventory Interpretation

0–10 This score suggests that you have a very small inner triangle and that you rely on external motivators in your decision-making. It also suggests that you need to build up your self-esteem, self-identity and self-respect. When you begin to actively and intentionally put effort into increasing these things, the end result will be personal growth and a larger triangle.

11–15 You have a solid foundation of self-worth upon which to begin creating your future. But you could probably benefit from putting some of your energy, time and talents into making your sense of self more positive. Even small changes in your attitudes and behaviors can have a major impact in what you decide to include in your dream life.

16–20 You are aware of what needs to be organized, remodeled, renovated or rebuilt in your life—or you have a pretty good hunch. You have what you need to start now, and you have what you need to continue enhancing your self-worth.

 What do your responses tell you about your current level of self-worth?

Is your self-worth high or low?

The statements in the Circle of Self-Inventory suggest a reliance on either internal or external sources of motivation. They also suggest traits of people with high and low levels of self-worth. The numbers you circled are statements that reflect reliance on internal motivation and a high level of self-worth. When you start assuming these positive behaviors and attitudes, you will begin to enhance your self-worth and feel more worthy of change. These functions of self-worth enhancement are grouped into easy-to-understand categories, or indicators.

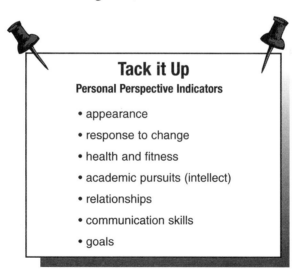

Tack it Up
Personal Perspective Indicators

- appearance
- response to change
- health and fitness
- academic pursuits (intellect)
- relationships
- communication skills
- goals

Note how these indicators are connected to your willingness to change. Can you recognize how your self-worth can be increased by paying attention to each indicator? For example, ask yourself how you can:

1. Improve your appearance.

2. Become more comfortable with change.

3. Enhance your health and fitness.

4. Engage your intellect.

5. Establish and maintain quality relationships.

6. Become a more effective communicator.

7. Establish goals consistent with your dream life.

The seven indicators above identify ways to increase your self-worth by increasing your reliance on internal motivators. By increasing one side of the equation, the other side increases. Action will lead to more action. The effect is often simultaneous, as a change in one indicator can apply to more than one inner circle, creating a crossover effect.

Inner Triangle = self-respect + self-identity + self-esteem

Built to Last

You (and only you) can determine which area(s) to address and how best to meet your personal needs. It is your responsibility to determine what courses of action, or strategies, will help you to achieve what is being asked. (I offer a few ideas because I just can't help myself.) Consider which approach on the following chart sounds best to you.

Indicator	What It Asks You to Consider	Ways to Do This
Appearance	Do you present yourself to the public in a way that is consistent with what you think about yourself?	*Treat yourself to a new outfit.*
	Do you like to look nice to please yourself rather than to please others?	*Get a new hair style.*
	How do you take care of your possessions and living environment?	*Clean out your closets.*
Change	How well do you respond to change?	*Go on an adventure.*
	Are you willing to initiate the needed changes in your life?	*Call a headhunter to explore job possibilities.*
	Do you assist or resist transition?	*Rearrange the furniture in your bedroom and see how that feels. Then rearrange the living room.*
	How willing are you to take risks that might have productive outcomes?	*Make an appointment with a counselor.*
	Are you willing to step out of what you know and learn more?	*Read another motivational book after you finish this one.*
Health/Fitness	Do you maintain a healthy lifestyle in which you eat well, get enough rest, exercise regularly, and engage in low-risk behaviors?	*Join a health club.*
	How would you describe your mental health?	*Stop listening to Dr. Laura.*
	Do you engage in protective behaviors like wearing a seatbelt when riding in a car?	*Get a new toothbrush, floss, observe the speed limit, look both ways before crossing the street and so on.*
	Do you get regular checkups?	*Call your doctor for an appointment.*
Intellect	How are your study or reading habits?	*Read a good book.*
	Are you excited about learning new things?	*Watch PBS.*
	Are you concerned about what's going on in the world around you?	*Subscribe to the morning paper rather than watch the local news.*

Relationships	How successful are you at building and maintaining relationships that are based upon mutual respect?	*Write a letter to someone whom you respect and ask him/her out to lunch—your treat.*
	Do you give the kind of friendship you want to receive?	*Send a friend a card— for no particular reason.*
	What role does drinking play in your relationships?	*Replace a nightcap or glass of wine with water or seltzer with a twist of lime.*
	Where do you go for help, guidance, and mentoring?	*Make a list of people you admire and why.*
	Are there people who can trust you as much as you trust them?	*Stop talking negatively or gossiping about anyone.*
Communication Skills	How often do you work on improving your ability to communicate?	*Read a book on assertiveness.*
	Do you know how to protect your own rights without violating the rights of others?	*Take an evening course in interpersonal communication.*
	Are you aware of what your body language communicates?	*One afternoon, observe people in a shopping mall. Record your observations.*
	What are you doing to enhance your perceptiveness?	*Practice giving feedback.*
Goals	What are your goals in life?	*Finish reading this book.*
	What are your aspirations; where do you see yourself in the future?	*Identify someone who is doing what you've always wanted to do; ask how they got there.*
	How do your goals influence your decision-making?	*Post daily goals on your fridge.*

How to Enhance Your Self-Worth

As you've just discovered, there are many ways to enhance your self-worth. You can never have enough positive self-perspective, despite what others may tell you. Cut out the "Build Me Ups" poster on the next page and place it where it will be a constant reminder of ways to enhance your self-worth.

Build Me Ups

Smile into your mirror every day and really look at who smiles back. Treat yourself to your favorite blend of coffee every morning. Say "Good morning" to complete strangers. Dress for success. Wear silly underwear. Hug a friend. Send your parents a thank-you card. Compliment a stranger. Make a list of your accomplishments. Learn to say "No" to things others want you to do and "Yes" to spending quiet time alone. Join a fitness club, and work out at least three times a week. Learn something new. Go to school. Go back to school. Read a book about your hobby. Browse through any *Chicken Soup for the Soul* book. Read *The Celestine Prophecy*, then look for coincidences in your own life. Sit in the front row of life—there will be plenty of available seats. Learn to forgive and forget. Take care of unfinished business. Get out of unhealthy relationships. Befriend people whom you admire. Become someone you admire. Read motivational books. Hang inspirational sayings in your home and office. Be positive. Avoid the word "but"—it takes you nowhere fast. Think instead of the word "build"—it will take you places.

Rely on yourself to make your life better. Figure out how to be your own most valuable resource by enhancing your sense of worth. When you do this you no longer have to worry about giving out the names of your favorite baby-sitter, housecleaner or carpenter. You are confident in your own ability to replace them with someone just as competent. Your friends will always ask for your recommendations. Count on it. Count on you.

Hitting The Nail on The Head

\ Change is easy. Believing you are worthy of change is the hard part.

\ Self-worth is made up of self-esteem, self-respect and self-identity, which are the three circles of The Inner Triangle.

\ The Inner Triangle concept suggests that the larger the circles, the larger your reliance on internal motivators, and vice versa.

\ True motivation comes from the inside out.

\ Self-worth can be enhanced by focusing on seven specific personal perspective indicators.

\ Take care of yourself because you can.

Making the Connection

> *Don't be fooled by the deceiver if the deceiver is*
> *always with you.*
>
> —Plato

If you asked yourself how to change your life, then gave a great answer, would you trust the information? When you don't have what it takes to feel deserving of life improvements, it's time to face the facts and work harder at building your self-worth (indicator by indicator), or change just isn't going to happen. Not only will change not happen, but you may continue to ignore the signs telling you that change is no longer an option—it's mandatory!

I admit that during the low tide period in my life, I wouldn't have hired me as my own self-worth builder. Although those who loved me continued to ask, "So, what do you want to do?" I continued to deny that change was needed. Instead of accepting my situation, I ignored it. What happens when you continue to look the other way—or forget to put yourself first—is that your behavior contradicts your words. You say one thing ("I'm fine") and then you do another (put your underwear on backwards).

So, what do you want to do?

What follows this kind of silliness or chaos is completely up to you. Either you can begin to recognize that your behavior is not in keeping with how you say you are doing, or you can own up to the fact that your everyday functioning is beginning to suffer. I realized that it was much easier to say everything was fine than admit to myself that my life needed some work. This realization was a reflection of my low self-worth at the time.

Although there are varying degrees of denial, you can assume for the sake of survival that there is a point—and maybe this is it—where you have to make the connection between the smaller incidents, mishaps and weirdness to the bigger picture. I know this isn't easy.

Consider a few of my behaviors prior to my realization that my life needed some repair. Does any of this sound familiar?

My Own Silliness

- While brewing morning coffee and doing a quick dusting of the house, I put the can of Pledge in the fridge instead of the creamer.
- I packed the car with the children's diaper bags, toys, and bottles to go grocery shopping and forgot to put the kids in the car.
- I went into the office and realized I hadn't brushed my hair that day.
- I paid the bills, then mailed them without putting the checks in the envelopes.
- I left the house wearing shoes that didn't match.
- I prepared macaroni and cheese from a box and forgot to add the cheese.
- I forgot where I put things around the house.
- I lost just about everything from keys to sunglasses on a daily basis.

If you were to compile your own list, what would be on it? It's okay not to have anything to write down. This suggests that you are doing better than most people are, and that's a good thing. But, given your high level of self-worth, you probably already knew that.

If, by chance, you have a long list, recognize that there are varying degrees of silliness, absentmindedness and stupidity in life, just as there are varying degrees of denial. This is an important distinction. You want to have control over your time. Otherwise, your life can spin away from you.

When you feel as if your life belongs to someone else or something else, you must first act to build your self-worth. You must come first before anyone or anything. This isn't selfish. This is survival. You will be of no use to those who depend upon you if you lose control over your own well being. Eventually, what may merely seem like internal confusion (silliness in behavior) can make you numb. I know from my own experience that after I stopped caring about my own happiness, I began to stop feeling. Unfortunately, this survival tactic only makes matters worse.

When your self-worth is dangerously lacking, you fail to act. You show up to your life, but you aren't capable of living it. Your body, however, continues to notice. It's obvious that when you have a constant headache, lower back pain, frequent gallbladder attacks or constant jaw trouble, something is wrong. So, you take something for the pain or have something removed. But what's wrong is still wrong.

> *The mind can only trick the heart for so long before the body jumps in to keep score.*

It's common to ask yourself, "Why work on enhancing my fitness when I can take a few painkillers? Why change my diet, seek psychological counseling or learn effective coping mechanisms when I can have my gallbladder removed or my jaw readjusted?" When your self-worth is low, you often look to someone else to fix your mistakes or repair the damage you've done. Although understandable, the opportunity to take back control of your life is lost. Not to mention that the person you look to for help could make things even worse!

Are there any physical signs suggesting a need for mastering your self-worth and initiating life-improvement changes?

Trust what your body is telling you. Listen to the natural signs. Trust what the silliness or chaos is telling you. In order to feel worthy of change, just look around! Even in the bad stuff that happens to you, there may be a calling for building your self-worth. Life will give you many different signs. It is your job to interpret their meaning.

When your self-worth is at a healthy level, for example, it's easier to see that being turned down for a promotion is an opportunity to develop new skills, find a new job or change your career altogether. When your self-worth is low, however, you interpret not being promoted as a bad thing. Believe that there are positive signs all around you, and spend some time interpreting what they are trying to tell you. Instead of complaining about a situation or a person, ask if that situation or person is really just a persistent wake-up call. You get 100 percent of energy every day. You can spend 20 percent of it complaining about your life, or spend that same 20 percent fixing it.

Now is a great time to stop and consider what has been happening in your life. Are there subtle or blatant signs suggesting that something needs to change? Is your sink leaking, and you still haven't called a plumber? Think of any frustrations, disappointments, successes, joys, roadblocks, sleeping habits, health problems, and so on that might be signs. If you are having trouble trying to determine or make sense out of the realities in your life, keep in mind that everyone has the same challenge. Some people are just better (and quicker) at dealing with the information. Others, having mastered the idea of self-worth, are just better at accepting what life has to offer. They move forward, having seen truth. Use the exercise on the next page, called "Flashing Signs," to help you see the truth.

So, what are you going to do with this information? The choice is yours. In Phase Two of The Future Plan, such information can be very helpful in determining what to include in your dream life—and what to delete. It can be the proverbial kick in the seat of your pants that will provide you with the motivation to learn how to build your self-worth as

FLASHING SIGNS

Directions: Place a checkmark next to each of the following that seems to imply that change is needed. Are these coincidences, or flashing signs?

_____ Nagging suspicion

_____ A wrong number

_____ A gut feeling

_____ Hearing from a long-lost friend

_____ Physical symptoms

_____ Constant headaches

_____ Fatigue

_____ Hyperactivity

_____ Back pain

_____ Sleeping difficulties

_____ Jaw clenching

_____ Nervous energy

_____ Relationships that take constant effort

_____ Not getting a promotion you thought you deserved

_____ An unexpected, joyous experience

_____ A billboard that you can't get out of your head

_____ A close call

_____ Working for a boss you can't stand

_____ Loss of a relative

_____ Loss of something valuable

_____ An accident or a near miss

_____ A chance encounter with someone that seems timely for some reason

_____ Something a child says to you

_____ Repeatedly fighting over the same thing or issue with someone

_____ A sentence from a book

well as give you a place to put your newfound talents to work. What follows is a story of how I saw a sign when my self-esteem was preventing me from moving forward.

The Calm After The Storm

We had just gotten our first major snowstorm in New England, and there were snow banks over four feet high on the corners of some streets. After dropping my kids off at day care, I found myself at an intersection where a little boy wearing a red knapsack stood waiting to cross the street on his way to school. I thought to myself, "Where's his mother?"

As I watched the little boy, I realized he wasn't going to cross this particular street without help. So I got out of my car and walked over to him. Before I even had a chance to speak, he looked up at me with big brown eyes that I'll never forget and said, "Hey lady, will you help me cross the street?" And then he smiled as I took his hand.

His touch broke through walls. His words became "Hey, Mommy, will you stay home with me?" When I closed my eyes during the nights that followed that incident, I saw the faces of my two young children looking up at me the same way the boy crossing the street had. From the inside out, I was beginning to hear what I needed to hear. It was time to quit my job and stay home with my children.

Quit. That four-letter word allowed me to make a number of other life-altering decisions. Believing in that little boy's message gave me permission to believe in my own happiness. It was time to listen. With this acceptance came an internal sense of calm after the storm.

Your Dream Life

Now it's time to put to use what you've learned up to this point. No longer can low self-worth hold you back. Forward momentum is pushing you to act, move and draw. Drawing the blueprints of your desired life is going to be an ongoing task, but there needs to be a starting point. This is it.

In Phase One you visualized your life as a house—as it stands today and were given the chance to draw it in Appendix A. To complete Phase Two you will again need to draw your life as a house, this time with the rooms reflecting how you *want* to be spending your time. Once again, a space has been reserved in the back of the book—Appendix B, "My Dream Life Drawing"—for you to record your thoughts, if you desire.

In preparing to draw your life the way you wish it looked today, remember that just because you have to include a particular room in your dream life drawing doesn't mean that it isn't part of your passion pursuit. Include what you have to do and what you want to do if this makes up your ideal life—however you choose to define it. Be more specific than in your first drawing (if you did one). Visualize the big picture. In this exercise, you want to answer the question, "If I could draw my life as if it were a house, what would it look like?" or "What do I want to wake up to every day?"

As in Phase One, make or envision the size and labels of your rooms reflective of your passions in life. The rooms in your dream house represent the roles that you either want to assume in life or that you, as we've discussed, have to assume as part of your responsibilities and commitments. Time remains the unit of measure, as it did for your first set of blueprints. One square equals one hour.

Live a little! Go for the essence of your dream life. You'll need a carpenter's pencil and Appendix B, "My Dream Life Drawing."

Back on The Curb

Now stand back on the curb and take a look at your drawing. What do you think? I'm assuming that some things are different from your first drawing, "My Life Now as a House" (found in Appendix A). Based upon your dream-life drawing, what needs to change in your life? Study your blueprints carefully. Think of all the possible things (life-improvement goals) that summarize your dream life. Remember, life-improvement goals include things like making more time for your children, having a career that you like, being healthy, living in another part of the country, traveling, and so on. Life-improvement goals are general and are made up of smaller objectives (called projects). You focus on one life-improvement goal at a time because they are so general.

> **Q** What are the greatest differences between your reality and your dream life?
>
> What needs to change in your life?

Based upon your answers to the above questions and your dream-life drawing, a few life-improvement goals can be identified. Because these goals will direct your future work, jot them down on the space provided below. You can have many goals or just one.

Even the happiest, most content people are always moving forward and finding new sources of joy. If you fall into this category, the drawings of your current and desired life will probably be different, just as if you needed to make significant life-improvement changes.

But no matter what your drawings look like, take time to reflect upon your life. The methods of The Future Plan don't work as quickly as it takes to read about them. It takes time to absorb all of the concepts and ideas of The Future Plan and then apply them to your life. Read about them now, but be open to making them part of your actions later on. Do the exercises as suggested, even though there may be times down the road when you can answer more honestly than now.

My Life-Improvement Goals

Directions: Make a list of major life goals below.

1. _____

2. _____

3. _____

4. _____

5. _____

The Future Plan is a program for bringing more meaning to your life. It's a five-phase process that offers guidance while you provide the expertise and labor. You can't build a new house overnight, just as you can't snap your fingers and have a new life. But you can start the process. You can move forward.

Don't worry about how to achieve one of the life-improvement goals you just identified; the next phase, Phase Three, "Defining the Scope of the Job," is all about creating options.

Hitting The Nail on The Head

There is a connection between feeling worthy of change and the ability to see the signs that change is needed.

Signs only have meaning when you are internally inspired to do something about what you read in them.

Ignoring signs that change is needed can be unhealthy.

Life-improvement goals result from the discrepancy between how you want to live your life and how you are living your life (Appendix B versus Appendix A).

Defining the Scope of Your Job

T he kitchen. This is where you are most likely to find a drawer whose only purpose is to store items like unsharpened pencils, blown fuses, half a box of used birthday candles, expired coupons, scraps of paper with phone numbers and no names, and a stick of stale gum. The only time you use this drawer is to put something else in it—not to take anything out. Why? Because it would take too much time to find what you are looking for in all the stuff that's crammed in there.

Your kitchen drawer is like your life. How many times have you decided to turn the drawer upside down into the trash? But something stops you. Are you afraid a hardware store will be closed when you need a picture hook, just like the one with the bent nail you threw out? Do you seriously think you'll ever chew that stick of gum? Or are you afraid of the freedom and control such an action would give you?

Replacing the known with the unknown is something most people resist doing. But if that resistance is not overcome, the result is inevitable—nothing changes. Phase Three takes your desire to improve your life and combines it with one life-improvement goal you identified at the end of the last chapter.

Phase 3

Define the Scope of Your Job

Purpose: *To plan how to accomplish your life-improvement goal by narrowing down the possibilities to realistic options, using a decision-making model.*

Phase Three is the planning and decision-making phase of The Future Plan. During this phase, you do not ask, "Will my life ever have meaning?" You explore answers to the question, "How do I make my life more meaningful?" You come up with lots of ideas (choices and actions). Then you select one life-improvement goal that seems most realistic.

To simplify this process, I give you four design-build categories to help you organize one life-improvement goal into four different levels of project risk.

Remember: quantity counts. Phase Three is where you generate as many possible project ideas as you can that would achieve the same life-improvement goal. Come up with the ideas first, and judge them later. From this point on, keep a pencil handy. Project ideas will pop up when you least expect them, and you'll want to write them down on the charts provided in Appendix C, "Design-Build Project Category Charts."

Once you start generating project ideas, it can be hard to stop! This phase of planning is filled with hope, possibility and discovery. Don't skip over the list making. Start focusing on the "how" of change. It's time to

Tack it Up

Design-Build Project Categories

1. Site Organization

2. Remodel

3. Renovate

4. Rebuild

believe in the possibilities. Start talking about your ideas with others. I prefer talking to strangers. They respond without any agenda or knowledge of me. I'll never see them again, so I have nothing to lose by previewing my ideas with them.

> *The more ways you can think of to make your passions part of your everyday life, the greater the odds a realistic solution will surface.*

Speak up! The more you talk about your ideas, the more real they will become to you. After a while, they won't seem so strange. Conversation helps define and refine your thoughts. You'll soon begin to hear yourself coming up with viable courses of action. Just remember, don't start with, "I know this will never happen, but ..."

Wait! There is risk in throwing out everything in your kitchen drawer. You might throw out the combination to the safe in your closet—if you actually put it in the drawer. So Phase Three is about creating alternatives based upon varying levels of risk, or project cost. This way, you are never without potential.

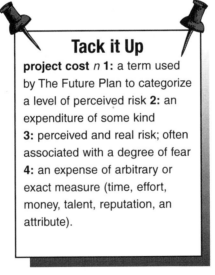

Tack it Up

project cost *n* **1:** a term used by The Future Plan to categorize a level of perceived risk **2:** an expenditure of some kind **3:** perceived and real risk; often associated with a degree of fear **4:** an expense of arbitrary or exact measure (time, effort, money, talent, reputation, an attribute).

The chart that follows summarizes the four design-build project options categorized by risk level. Whether your design-build project affects others will raise the risk level. After all, there is more at stake when your decisions impinge on someone else's life.

Design-Build Project Categories

Level	Design-Build Category	Description	Project Cost (Risk Level)	Involves Others?
1	Site Organization	Clean up; throw out; organize; declutter	None to low	No
2	Remodel	Alter an existing structure; fix up	Low to moderate	Occasionally
3	Renovation	Add a new structure; remove an existing structure	Moderate to high	Usually
4	Rebuild	Start over; build from the bottom up; relocate	High	Yes

Keep in mind, too, that no one is looking over your shoulder or second-guessing your creative genius. So go for what you want! You are in complete control. Each of the design-build project categories is explained in more detail below. When you are ready to fill in your own charts, simply turn to Appendix C and begin.

To enhance your understanding of each category, however, a sample life-improvement goal is also provided on the following pages. It is "to achieve a healthier lifestyle." It's general, easy to break down into smaller projects, and represents the essence of the change needed. You will use just one life-improvement goal throughout all the design-build project categories in Appendix C.

> *Always clean up a job site at the end of the day.*
> *It shows you how much you've accomplished and*
> *prepares you for the next day.*
>
> —Thomas Denney

Level 1: Site Organization

This is the first level of design-build project options. It involves getting your act together. This can mean anything from letting go of the physical and the imagined (giving away possessions or letting go of your limiting beliefs or attitudes) to adding on to your life (developing new systems for efficiency or assuming a new outlook on life). Actions or changes that have little or no effect on other people, yet allow you to feel more organized and in control of your life, belong in Level 1.

Even though actions of Level 1 may seem insignificant, they become more important when you consider their effects over time. Making your site (life) organized and neat allows you to see where you are going and points the way to greater changes. It makes room for assessment and frees up space.

Because the kinds of things you do in Level 1 are small in scope, you can often do more than one project at a time. You can work on pouring a strong foundation for larger projects, or find daily renewal in the simple things in life. Some projects will be one-shot deals; others may be ongoing.

Example of Site Organization

Life Goal: *To live a healthier lifestyle*

Project Ideas

✓ Walk every day before taking your shower.

✓ Drink eight glasses of water a day.

✓ Stop drinking soda.

✓ Floss after every meal.

✓ Take a daily vitamin.

✓ Have an annual physical.

> *The more valuable your possessions were to you at one time, the greater the gift to someone else.*

To understand the value of letting go, consider the fact that whenever my husband the handyman starts a home-improvement project, he gets a dumpster. The size or scope of the job doesn't matter because dumpsters come in varying sizes. The bigger the dumpster, though, the greater the appearance that there's a lot of work being done.

Big dumpsters attract neighbors and friends you haven't seen for months, who arrive with stuff to throw in your dumpster! All of a sudden they, too, have things in their lives they'd like to let go—and guess where they want to put it?

Level 1 can be viewed as one big dumpster. It asks the question, "What can you do without?" It asks you to explore what needs figuratively and literally to be thrown out, cleaned up or sorted through.

Specifically, Level 1 can be viewed as the opportunity to do one big spring cleaning. The dumpster can stay, too. As you prepare to take greater levels of risk and get your life back under control, start cleaning! Clean out your closets. Organize your office. Get rid of clothes you haven't worn in a year. Give away books, dishes, coats, collections and other things that remind you how much is just taking up space in your life rather than giving it more meaning.

Decluttering your physical environment will have a significant impact on your sense of order. Every time you open a drawer, reach for a shirt, or make your bed, you see there is organization in your life. Throw out the contents of your kitchen drawer and rejoice in your new-found sense of control. Declutter your life. Wow!

Let things go mentally, too. Stop worrying about what other people think and allow yourself some space to grow. Your negative thoughts, poor attitude, low self-worth and that chip on your shoulder—if they exist—can all go in the dumpster. So can your desire to procrastinate. Take care of the little things around you that need your attention, like balancing your checkbook. Part of letting go is recognizing your bad habits (we all have them).

What about adding on? Deciding to use your brain power to make your day more efficient is one way to organize your life. For instance, by getting up an hour earlier every morning, you could work out or take a walk before you start your daily routine. By adding something to your daily routine (even saying "I love you" every day to your significant other), you take ownership of your perceptions and attitudes. This is an important building block for higher level projects.

Level 2: Remodel

This is the second level of design-build project categories, where you fix up, make better, repair or remake one or more existing structures in your life. You are taking something that already exists—such as an attitude or belief—and altering it. As a result, your behaviors (communication skills, recreational pursuits, sense of obligations), involvements (job responsibilities, civic duties, volunteer work) and relationships are also remodeled or made different. Others have to make adjustments in how they respond to you. This fact increases the risk level.

Others may become involved in your projects by default or by design. And remaking your life may require the expertise of others. Don't shy away from potential connections and resources. A Level 2 project idea can be to ask someone to help you reach your life-improvement goal.

Example of Remodeling

Life Goal: To live a healthier lifestyle

Project Ideas

✓ Get The Patch and cut down on smoking.

✓ Alter your diet to include less fat.

✓ Walk with friends on a regular basis.

✓ Attend an aerobics class four times a week.

✓ Convert the space over the garage into a gym.

✓ Train to run in a five-mile road race.

✓ Resign from a committee at work that is stressful.

✓ Leave for work earlier so you can drive within the speed limit.

Behaviors

Attitude changes usually result in behavioral changes; the two are connected and can operate in both directions. If you want to alter the way you think about yourself, and thus how you allow others to treat you, it might be fitting in Level 2 to start saying "No" more often. In your attempt to remake your identity, you might also find it useful at this level to pull the plug on the neon "Kick Me!" sign that's been on your back for years. Both are examples of how you can create your future by making adjustments in how you communicate. Conversely, such a discovery (learning how to be assertive) may force other people to modify how they treat you.

Learning how to delegate responsibility, accepting that good can sometimes be good enough, taking time off from work, reducing or increasing the hours you work per week, or renegotiating your allocation of domestic duties are additional examples of behaviors found in the Level 2 design-build project category.

Involvements

Another way this design-build project category can help you achieve your life-improvement goal is by suggesting the benefit of becoming involved (or more involved) in things that are already part of your life in some way or have a low project cost. Let's say you want to remodel your soul. One way to do so would be to increase your involvement in your local church—maybe even to join the church choir. Depending upon how well you sing, this may be risky for the other choir members! To join the choir might also require other minor adjustments, like hiring a baby-sitter, checking your spouse's schedule and practicing in the shower. Remember, Level 2 changes often bring others into your effort.

Consider becoming involved in formal and informal organizations related to your current interests, such as clubs, social groups, support groups, educational classes, interest groups, health clubs, investment groups, diet centers, community groups and job-related committees. Although there will be some crossover between these activities and the next design-build project category, as long as the project idea is related to something you are already doing—or is part of your existing structure—and the project cost is low to moderate in your view, such ideas fit this level.

Are there people in your life who bring you down, not up?

Relationships

Finally, examination of your current relationships is a significant function of Level 2 projects.

Some human relationships are hard; some are easy. Some are good for you; some are harmful. Some help take you where you want to go; others block your way. Taking the time and energy to determine the way you feel about your relationships allows you take ownership of how you spend your time (and life). However, relationships are clearly not things that can simply be discarded, like a broken armchair, tossed into a dumpster or put at the curb for trash pickup. Consideration of the feelings of others is part of your examination process.

Level 3: Renovate

This is the third level of design-build project categories. It involves adding or deleting significant aspects of your life that are directly related to the pursuit of your passion. To renovate your life is to make or create more time for the pursuit of your passions. Project ideas at this level usually involve others and are noticeable. That's one reason it's such an exciting option. The new you gets noticed! People will begin to comment on your efforts and provide the recognition you need to keep it up. (A little external motivation never hurt anyone!)

At Level 3 you choose project ideas that are comparable to adding a new room or removing a room in your life's blueprints. You're not expanding an existing aspect of your life—you are creating one or making a significant one go away.

> **Example of Renovating**
>
> **Life Goal:** *To live a healthier lifestyle*
>
> **Project Ideas**
>
> ✓ Quit drinking.
>
> ✓ Stop smoking.
>
> ✓ Seek marriage counseling.
>
> ✓ Sell property to buy sailboat.
>
> ✓ Join a weekly ski-racing team.
>
> ✓ Take a six-month sabbatical to train for a triathlon.

Another distinguishing factor of the Level 3 design-build project category is the project cost. There is a moderate to high level of risk associated with making such significant life changes. You are spending more resources with the intent of more directly pursuing your passions—resources such as time, energy and your talents. To be comfortable with this level of risk, you must believe that you are worthy of achieving your life-improvement goal.

For Level 3 projects, you will need to accept that there is a much greater consequence associated with your choices. More is done away with or added. Becoming a licensed flying instructor or selling property to buy a sailboat to pursue your love of sailing are examples of Level 3 project ideas.

Not all dream lives are made up of the pursuit of a passion. Leaving an abusive relationship, quitting your job to care for an elderly parent, or taking in a foster child are also examples of Level 3 project ideas. These projects are based on the premise that passion can be found in everything you do—especially in what you do for others. Remember, passion is the power behind your actions.

> *You often have to take things down before you can build them up again.*

Level 4: Rebuild

This is the fourth and final level of design-build project categories. It represents a new start, or your desire to build from the ground up. This category of risk is summed up by the phrase, "Go for it!" With Level 4 design-build projects, there's usually no turning back. You can turn in a different direction, but once you've quit a job, sold your home, adopted a child from Romania or canceled your engagement party, you're committed to something new. You've torn down your old house, and you have to build or find a new place to live. For this reason, attempting only one Level 4 project at a time is recommended.

You can make adjustments or change your plans once you see how things are progressing. You can cut back or build something bigger. The one thing you probably can't do, though, is go back to the way things were before you rolled up your sleeves and set the wrecking ball in motion. Even if you tried to recreate the status quo, it wouldn't be the same. But isn't that the point?

Example of Rebuilding

Life Goal: To live a healthier lifestyle

Project Ideas

✓ Become a spokesperson for an anti-smoking campaign.

✓ Find religion.

✓ Leave a dysfunctional or abusive relationship.

✓ Hire a personal trainer on an annual basis.

✓ Train full-time for the Iron Man competition.

✓ Become a vegetarian.

✓ Take a year off and sail around the world.

✓ Invite your parents to live with you.

Level 4 projects usually bring some degree of anxiety for those you care about, as they wonder how they will deal with the new you. One of the risks in the rebuild option is that the lives of others are significantly affected by your choices. Projects in this category are big. A hard hat is required. In fact, more than one hard hat may be required, for the people close to you.

Also accompanying Level 4 design-build options is a renewed sense of freedom. Project ideas in this high-cost project category can make you feel alive again. Building your own business from the ground up, deciding to start a family or selling your home and moving to Africa to work for the Peace Corps are Level 4 project ideas that undoubtedly change your life forever. The freedom that accompanies the process of considering this level of design-build project categories can be energizing in and of itself.

If you choose a project in a Level 4 category—after considering all of the potential consequences and having all of the necessary conversations any reasonable person could expect to have prior to breaking ground—give yourself credit for the level of self-worth it took to "go for it!" Don't lose that by leaving your project half-completed or by giving up when things don't go quite as planned. For instance, if you discover that quitting your job and trying to find one directly related to your passion isn't happening overnight, then make adjustments to your plan. But don't give up on your life-improvement goal.

Helpful Reminder

As you generate lists of project ideas on the charts provided in Appendix C, ask yourself, "How do I surround my life with what brings me pleasure?" Also ask, "What could I do to be spending more of my time the way I want to be spending it?" Recall that life-improvement goals are accomplished through projects. Projects describe the specific work to be done to help you to achieve your life-improvement goal. What follows is an example of project ideas of increasing risk, as I perceive risk. For this example, the passion being pursued is the love of golf.

Life is like golf. You can't always see what you're aiming for—but you know
you're playing the game.

Life-Improvement Goal: To pursue a passion for golf

Project Ideas

Design-Build Level 1

- Volunteer to work at a professional tournament.
- Clean your golf clubs.
- Subscribe to a golf magazine.
- Practice putting in your backyard before work.
- Take an annual golf vacation.

Design-Build Level 2

- Have weekend golf outings (which can include the entire family).
- Write articles about golf and submit them for publication.
- Volunteer to offer golf lessons at your local YMCA or high school.
- Organize a community golf outing to benefit your local library.

Design-Build Level 3

- Sign up for weekly golf lessons.
- Set aside one night a week as your golf night.
- Become a starter at your local golf course.

Design-Build Level 4

- Build a house next to a golf course and move there.
- Become a professional caddy.
- Invent a board game about golf and quit your job to promote it.
- Teach your significant other to play golf.

These examples illustrate the many ways to pursue a passion for the game of golf through project ideas. The Future Plan is designed to be practical—that's why where you place your project ideas is so important. Given your personal situation, at what level do your project ideas belong?

Tack it Up

Tips for Creating Project Ideas

- Work with only one life-improvement goal (the same one for each level).
- Come up with as many project ideas as you wish.
- Make your project ideas as crazy or far out as you want.
- There is no right and wrong, up and down, or front and back.
- Don't think about reality yet; think about your dream.
- Go for a quantity of ideas.
- Focus on the "how" and not on the "if."

Don't get caught up in the "what ifs" and risks associated with change or doing something as daring as throwing out your kitchen drawer—throw it out! Dump it! Odds are the clutter in your life is taking up valuable space. Be selfish in your pursuit of ways to achieve a more meaningful life.

Hitting The Nail on The Head

\ Phase Three of The Future Plan provides four design-build project options, with different levels of risk.

\ The goal of Phase Three is to generate lists of project ideas in Appendix C.

\ A quantity of ideas will produce quality planning.

\ Small changes can serve as a strong foundation for larger changes in life.

\ There is no greater freedom than the freedom to create your future.

10

Decision Making 101

I think that indecisiveness might just be a decision...
maybe.

H aving incomplete projects around your house can be frustrating. They serve as a constant reminder that you aren't in control. Every time you rip a coat on your broken screen door, trip over twelve pairs of shoes waiting to be dropped off at the Salvation Army, or pull faded curtains shut in your bedroom, your decisions not to act become obvious. Maybe you just haven't gotten around to it. Maybe you don't feel you have the time. Or you just don't know where to start. There's too much to do, too many decisions to make.

Making decisions does not have to be difficult. The more choices you have, the more exciting the process and the better the potential outcome. Take a moment now to warm up to making a decision about which design-build category you will pursue in the next phase of The Future Plan.

The decision-making model that I have developed uses five factors. Realistically, however, they might not encompass all of your personal circumstances. There may be considerations or factors that you—and only you—need to take into account when selecting what level of risk makes sense. For example, what is your health status? Do you have family expectations or demands on your time, previous commitments or future commitments, relationship issues to consider, or financial obligations that will affect your decision making?

These kinds of questions, and others, need your attention before you choose a design-build project category. Your answers will determine the degree of change you can realistically assume in your life. You still maintain control, yet are working within your reality. Everyone has personal considerations that affect their choices in life. Freedom does not preclude having to make choices or weigh factors.

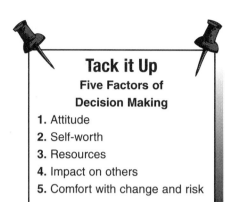

Tack it Up

Five Factors of
Decision Making

1. Attitude
2. Self-worth
3. Resources
4. Impact on others
5. Comfort with change and risk

The decision-making model offered with The Future Plan is easy to use. It narrows your list of potential projects to only one design-build project category. It helps you to determine the scope of your job based upon five —and only five— factors. Although each of these factors can be broken down even further, it is your general feeling about each factor that should guide your decision making—your initial reaction to each consideration is what should guide your selections.

After you finish this book, you can (and should) return to the decision-making model to see if you want to make adjustments. You can also continue to record new project ideas on the charts in Appendix C. Use the rulers on the next few pages to help assess which design-build category holds realistic project ideas for you to pursue. Place a check mark directly on the measurement that matches your assessment. Circle only whole numbers (i.e., 1, 2, 3, 4 or 5). This will make your final number easier to calculate.

Attitude

Your outlook on life, or attitude, is the most significant consideration that will make or break the pursuit of your life-improvement goal. Without a positive outlook, the process of creating your future becomes sabotaged before you even begin. Self-created limiting beliefs take over, and you're left with a sense of hopelessness. As a tennis fan, I can't help but agree with Andre Agassi when he says, "Attitude is everything." If you believe in your ability to achieve your dream, you will. Ask "How?" to make your goal a reality, not "If" it will ever happen.

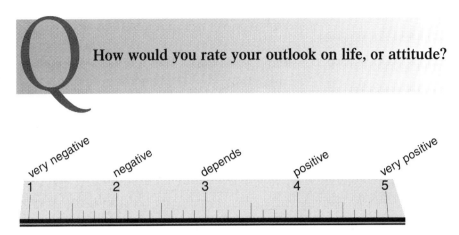

How would you rate your outlook on life, or attitude?

Self-worth

Feeling worthy to achieve your dreams and pursue your passions serves as a significant source of internal motivation. Your level of self-worth needs to include a healthy level of self-esteem, self-identity and self-respect for you to change.

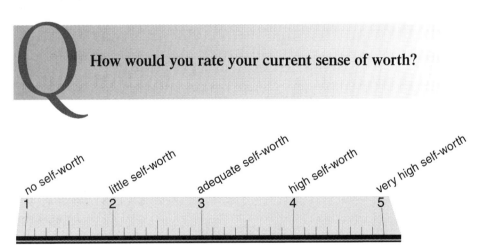

How would you rate your current sense of worth?

Resources

There are many different kinds of resources that can help you complete your projects. Being able to afford the pursuit of your passion depends upon how you define the term "resource." For example, time, personal contacts, financial assets, skills, personality, access to various opportunities, reputation, intelligence, family, talent and so on all provide you with a potential means of accomplishing your goal. It's easy to believe that money is the most important resource, but it's not. As you'll see later, you are richer than you think.

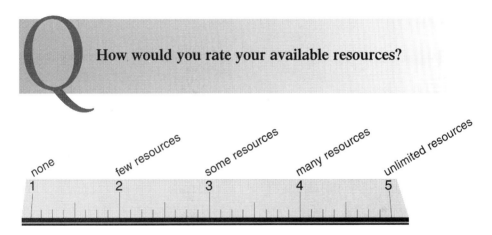

Impact on Others

Your life does not happen in a vacuum. What you choose to do has an impact on others. You interact with others and they with you; you may also provide for others. This affects your decision making. Who demands use of your time? Who needs you, and whom do you need? Family, friends, colleagues, employees, employers and anyone else who can potentially be affected by changes in your life should be taken into consideration when choosing a design-build project category.

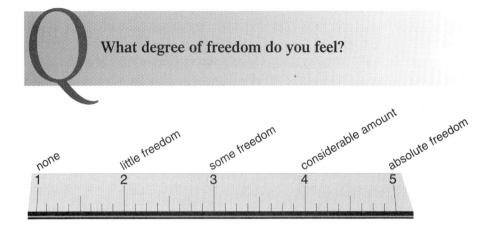

Q What degree of freedom do you feel?

none	little freedom	some freedom	considerable amount	absolute freedom
1	2	3	4	5

"Oops! I got carried away."

Comfort with Change and Risk

Being comfortable with change and risk is one of the most revealing measures of your true intentions. Regardless of your past feelings about changing your life, what you desire to do today is what counts. If you feel inspired to overcome any potential fears associated with change itself, you will. Your rating should reflect your future, not your past. Taking the risks that accompany change is part of the change process.

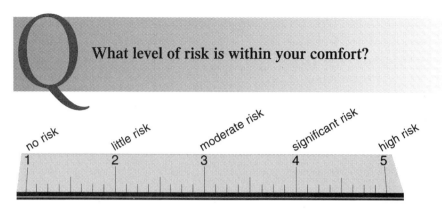

What level of risk is within your comfort?

no risk • little risk • moderate risk • significant risk • high risk

1 • 2 • 3 • 4 • 5

Every day that passes in which you choose not to take action towards your life-improvement goal is a day you don't get back. Your future is now. To determine the design-build category in which to begin in Phase Four, simply transfer your ratings (i.e. 1, 2, 3, 4 or 5) from each ruler to its corresponding column on the chart that follows. Then add up all five of these numbers. Divide by five. The resulting number tells you which design-build category holds the most realistic project ideas for you to pursue. You've already made lists of project ideas under all four design-build project categories— now, you've eliminated three of them.

Design-Build Decision-Making Process

Attitude	Self worth	Resources	Impact/ Involvement	Change/ Risk
1	1	1	1	1
2	2	2	2	2
3	3	3	3	3
4	4	4	4	4
5	5	5	5	5

Number Circled:

_____ _____ _____ _____ _____ = _____
(Total)

Divide Total by 5 = _____ (Average Rating)

If your Average Rating equals:	Use project ideas in this design-build project category:
1.0 to 1.5	Site Organization
1.6 to 2.5	Remodel
2.6 to 3.5	Renovate
3.6 to 5.0	Rebuild

Although different values may be assigned to your responses, the purpose of this decision-making process is to demonstrate that you have the information you need to begin your work. You've got what it takes to do *something,* whether it is a Site Organization or a Rebuild design-build project. There is at least one project, in your lists of project ideas (Appendix C) that will improve your life. This is also where you will find the answer to the question, "So, what do you want to do?"

Regardless of which design-build category you choose, remember that you will have to spend something in order to get something. The more energy, time and action you put into seeking your passion, the more likely it will become a reality. The more thought that goes into your decision-making before you act, the better your chances for making a good decision.

A Father with a Dilemma

For weeks and weeks, he agonized over what to do. Should he take the job? Should he not take the job? This father of two was caught on the horns of a dilemma.

The job being offered would make him a major player, almost double his salary and give him immediate prestige and power. They were making him an offer he couldn't refuse—or so he thought. He had researched the prospective company on the Internet. He had checked with people who knew people who knew people at the prospective company. He had considered the opportunities he had at his present place of employment. With one more conversation, the father would have all of the information he needed to make his decision—a good decision.

When he got home from work that night, he joined his family at the dinner table. Seeing his father's worried face, his son asked, "What's the matter?" After he explained the dilemma, the son looked at his father and asked, "So, which job gets you home for dinner earlier?" The father replied, "The job I have now." To this his son said, "Guess you know what to do then."

Remember!

You will be held accountable for decisions and actions that result from The Future Plan. Every move you make from this point on is intentional, or by design. So anticipate. Be prepared. Get a dumpster— your own dumpster. (You don't want to be on the receiving end of someone else's dumpster obsession.) Spend the money. You may not think you will need it, but even the smallest of jobs requires letting some stuff go.

As previously suggested, just getting rid of material possessions, obsessions, destructive attitudes, low self-worth and so on is one way of gaining back some degree of order and control over your life. Even Level 1 design-build projects remind you that small things do matter. Start projects you can complete.

Half-finished projects in your life are frustrating. The goal of The Future Plan is to start what you finish by selecting a design-build category that you can handle. Start small to ensure success or go for it if you are able to work with higher risk. You have a place to begin your work— a design-build category containing project ideas. Now it's time to get to work! It's time to begin Phase Four.

Hitting The Nail on The Head

\ There are five essential factors involved in selecting a design-build project category.

\ Your personal circumstances do matter in your decision-making.

\ You can eliminate three potential design-build project categories (leaving just one) using an effective, yet simple, decision-making model.

\ Start projects you can finish.

Begin Your Work

Assume for a moment that you've decided to remodel your kitchen. This one remodeling project disrupts all other aspects of your life—there's no getting around it. Life becomes different and difficult as other rooms in your home become multifunctional. Your bathroom, for instance, becomes part-kitchen—your pots and pans, dishes, silverware and glassware are stacked in the bathtub. Nonperishable food items are stored in a cardboard box in the living room. Your can opener is hung on the front hall doorknob. Empty jugs of water are shoved in next to your cleaning supplies, and your coffeepot shares the same outlet in the bathroom as your electric toothbrush. As my daughter would say, you are in a complete state of "dish-come-bob-elation."

As you sip your morning coffee in the bathroom, you notice it has a minty fresh taste to it. You wonder if things will ever return to normal. Lately, your last thought before falling asleep at night is "What have I done?"

The decision to make your life more meaningful will undoubtedly lead to a little chaos. If you aren't willing to get a little dirty or into a state of "dish-come-bob-elation" once in a while, you aren't going to make any life improvements. You won't be willing to act to achieve your dreams. This is why Phase Four is the best place to don a pair of overalls.

Granted, overalls weren't designed to enhance your figure. In fact, I believe they were invented as a place to store stuff—including your figure. You can hang a hammer from the right-side leg loop. You can slip a screwdriver into the deep pocket on your left side. Your submarine sandwich fits nicely in your lower right-hand pocket. You can store a half-pound of nails in the far right bib, which won't even touch the other half-pound of nails in the center bib. To avoid looking lopsided, the far left bib pocket is perfect for screws. The fact that John Glenn probably had an easier time walking around in his first space suit than you in your overalls isn't important. Overalls are necessary in Phase Four. They make more than a fashion statement. They help you accept the fact that to complete your projects—to change—you will have to do some physical work. You will have to get dirty.

Whether you decide to organize, remodel, renovate, or rebuild your life, expect to make a mess along the way. You are changing. Things around you will become displaced, mixed up, and different. But change only happens when you act.

Phase 4

Begin Your Work

Purpose: *To decide how to carry out your projects; to get to work.*

The purpose of Phase Four is to identify starting points. Ask yourself, "What do I need to do, in what order, and by when?" Part of this action phase involves putting your carpenter's pencil to work to create "to do" lists or what The Future Plan calls "punch lists." Pages of blank "to do" lists are found in Appendix D. When you figure out how to accomplish a particular project idea, jot it down before you forget.

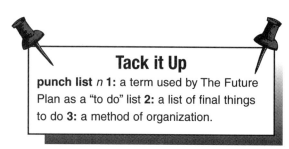

Tack it Up

punch list *n* **1:** a term used by The Future Plan as a "to do" list **2:** a list of final things to do **3:** a method of organization.

Every time you accomplish one of the actions on your "to do" list, you can cross it off. Every time you need to add an action to your punch list, you can add it. Keep returning to your punch list as you get more and more ideas about how to accomplish a particular project. A sample punch list is found below for the project idea "to walk on a regular basis." Although there are numerous other project ideas to reach the life-improvement goal, "to become more physically fit," only one is illustrated.

Sample Punch List

Life-Improvement Goal: To become more physically fit.
Project Idea: To walk on a regular basis.

Priority	To Do List	Begin	End	✓
2	Identify someone to walk with me (and my dog) five times a week.	_____	_____	_____
3	Call this person. Talk to dog.	_____	_____	_____
4	Call the person to confirm the time and dates for the walk week.	_____	_____	_____
1	Go to the store and buy a good pair of running shoes, a strong leash and a water bottle.	_____	_____	_____
5	Walk for forty minutes.	_____	_____	_____

As you can see, some actions will need to proceed other actions. For this reason, your punch list has a place to prioritize your actions. It also has a place to write in when you have to begin—and finish—doing something. The deadline is the most effective external source of motivation. It represents the death, termination and extinction of your desire to procrastinate or to take no action.

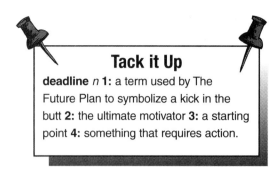

Tack it Up

deadline *n* **1:** a term used by The Future Plan to symbolize a kick in the butt **2:** the ultimate motivator **3:** a starting point **4:** something that requires action.

A deadline allows you to work backwards and determine timelines for your action items. Without closure, you may never finish your project. You might never start it, either. Good, bad or indifferent, change will require the use of deadlines because deadlines force you to act.

Keep in mind that self-imposed deadlines are effective to the extent that you take them seriously. By enlisting someone or something else to reinforce your self-imposed deadline, you are more likely to follow through. You are more likely to act.

Action

Action is the expenditure of energy required to move one force against another. To bring more meaning into your life or to build your dream life, you are going to physically have to do something. There are many kinds of movements that constitute action in Phase Four. You may not realize it, but reading this book is an example of one force working against another—of your taking action.

To act is to do, to perform, to make a mess. Although I try to be neat (albeit not very hard), I'm what you'd call "organizationally impaired." Making a mess doesn't really bother me. I thrive on clutter. I relish not being able to find two matching socks. Spending twenty minutes every morning looking for the kids' sneakers is time built into my morning routine. When I reach into the cupboard to get one Tupperware container, they all come tumbling down. I have to conscientiously make an effort to get my act together on a daily basis. I like to think it is because I'm spontaneous and impulsive. Getting organized to act—and then acting—is exactly what you do in Phase Four. Becoming organized is your first job. Even the most organizationally impaired individuals can get through this phase. After all, I did.

"Making life improvements is exhilarating—or do I mean exhausting?"

Simplify and Focus

Trying to do too many home improvements at once usually means that none of them actually get completed. This highlights the need to simplify and focus. Once you have gone through the process of filling out punch list after punch list, you need to actually do your punch lists— one action item at a time. Avoid getting sidetracked or misled because that means that you are trying to do too much or going in too many directions at once.

Don't retreat if someone challenges your motives. Don't throw in the towel after you run out of coffee. Don't give up on your dreams when your dog eats your paint brush. Stay focused on your goal. Manage your time accordingly. Say "No" to requests for time that will take you away from your project. Get away from stuff that is too time-consuming and not a priority. Give yourself the time you need to work on your projects.

How can you simplify your life and stay focused on your goal?

The end product of Phase Four is completion of your punch lists. This will take some time. But, there's no turning back now. You not only have a plan, but your plan is well-thought-out, reflects your true passions, and is realistic. When you discover a new way of achieving a more meaningful life Bam! you are different.

Jake's BAM! Theory

One day after kindergarten Jake came running into the house with a handful of worms. His eyes were wide with excitement, and he had a spring in his step. After tracking me down, he said, "Look Mommy, I just figured out something really important." Having sparked my curiosity, I moved closer to him and then noticed he was holding a handful of worms.

"Oh!" I exclaimed and took a few steps back.

Jake said, "Mommy, look what I just discovered. When I squeeze my hand really hard— BAM!—some of the worms get squished, but some of them just fall on the floor and crawl away!"

Jake got into the habit of shouting with enthusiasm, "BAM!" whenever he discovered that one action led to another. I soon learned to be prepared to respond with an equal amount of enthusiasm—and 409 household cleaner. After his squeezing-the-worms discovery, Jake found almost one thing a day worthy of a "BAM!" or two.

Late one afternoon, for instance, Jake came running downstairs. He yelled, "Mommy, I've figured something else out." I quickly came running. "When you eat chocolate ice cream on the white couch," Jake began, "BAM! It doesn't come off."

Less than a week later, after hours of suspiciously little fighting between Jake and his younger sister, I again heard, "BAM! I figured it out." I ran to the kids. "It's true," Jake said. "If you leave the cat locked in the closet long enough—BAM! She will pee in there."

There is no denying the cause and effect connection. There is no denying how actions lead to change.

Bless This Mess

There's no reason why you can't achieve your dream life or add more meaning to your life. There's also no reason why you can't change your plans if you need to. After all, it's been my experience that a wrench or two may come flying in your direction during your work. The first thing to do is duck. The second is to be willing and able to change your plans—even switch to a different project—if what you are doing isn't working.

Just because you can't proceed as you originally thought doesn't mean you shouldn't proceed. If you knock down a wall and find a spider web of wires behind it, you really have no choice but to hire an electrician. Acting as if the wires aren't there isn't productive. You can't control or predict the future. Have a plan—just be willing to accommodate the unexpected.

There will be limits to how much you can change your life all at once. Only you can accurately assess those limits. I must admit that when it comes to home improvement projects, I take on more than I can finish. I start in one room and, before you know it, the entire house is in a state of "dish-come-bob-elation." Wallpaper is half-stripped. Walls are half-painted. Furniture is stacked in the hallway. Light fixtures are detached from the ceiling. And—yes—dishes, pots and pans are in the bathtub. My projects often remain half-done until someone (guess who?) gets so disgusted that he steps in and finishes the job (a home-improvement strategy that has worked for me over the years).

Nonetheless, I caution you about making your first project as potentially disruptive as renovating your kitchen. Consider the pros and cons of initiating mass chaos your first time through The Future Plan. Before you know it, you might find nothing wrong with eating your morning cereal out of the box it came in. You might discover that your hallway doorknob is a rather convenient place to keep your can opener. Although these may be worthwhile discoveries, you've created a mess without creating progress. Phase Four is designed to move you forward.

Phase Five is presented in the next chapter. This is the final phase of The Future Plan. It is the phase of evaluation and inspection. It is the phase that requires a few new tools —especially a flashlight...

The Future Plan Progress Report

Activity:	The Future Plan:
• Look at how I spend my time.	Phase One
• Explored how I want to spend my time.	Phase Two
• Make lists of life-improvement goals.	Phase Two
• Narrow list down to one life-improvement goal.	Phase Two
• Create Project ideas in all four levels of risk for achieving life-improvement goal.	Phase Three
• Choose a decision-build project category using decision making model.	Phase Three
• Make a punch list containing action items for each project idea.	Phase Four
• Establish deadlines.	Phase Four
• Carry out, add and delete action items.	Phase Four
• Check your progress	Phase Five
• Look at how you now spend your time.	Phase Five

Hitting The Nail on The Head

\\ Phase Four is the action phase.

\\ Effective planning ensures the completion of your work in Phase Four.

\\ Punch lists are "to do" lists.

\\ Completing one project at a time allows you to simplify and focus on reaching your life-improvement goal.

\\ Plan on changing your plans.

\\ Start only what you can finish.

\\ Change happens over time.

12

Life Inspection

The exterior appearance can hide the interior truth.

By now it's obvious. I like comparing seemingly unrelated objects to one another as a means of altering what I might see. For instance, this book uses a life as house analogy to suggest that making your life have more meaning doesn't have to be as complicated as it first appears. In fact, it can be somewhat fun (even entertaining), when you start thinking in terms of organizing, remodeling, renovating or completely rebuilding your life from the ground up. Maybe it's the distance—or freedom—offered by comparing two distinctly different things using "like" or "as" that makes reality less threatening. Take evaluation, for instance.

Being effective and honest about where The Future Plan will take you (or has taken you) is like walking around in the dark holding a flashlight. Sure, you assume your flashlight has batteries—working batteries—so you can see in front of you or behind you. This assumption often leaves you in the dark, tripping over sneakers, chairs and the dog.

There's no denying the diversity, accessibility and usefulness of a flashlight. Maybe that's why everyone has one—just not one that always works. You will need a working flashlight (one with charged batteries) for Phase Five of The Future Plan, "Inspect Your Work," because a flashlight allows you to see into dark places—into corners, around pipes and under beams. It can reveal the stuff in your life (house) that you may have missed up to this point. Without the ability to look closely at what's around you, your ability as a home inspector is compromised. (It doesn't count just to have a flashlight in your hand—if you've taken out the batteries, the odds of illumination are slim to none!)

Phase 5

Inspect Your Work

Purpose: *To identify what's been done and what's left to do.*

Phase Five is an on-going process. It represents the continual process of walking around your life to see if you like what you've done to your place. While you are achieving one life-improvement goal, you can be inspecting your progress. You don't have to wait until it is completely finished; it never really is. Life goes on with days blending into days, which often makes it hard to identify a clear-cut completion date. But you can get a sense of how you've done and how you feel about your future.

Phase Five answers the questions, "Have I gotten what I want?" and "What in my life still needs to be organized, remodeled, renovated or rebuilt?"

As a result of completing Phase Five, you may discover and see things you've suspected all along but weren't ready to accept. Now that you've actually done something as selfish (and deserving) as planning your life-improvement goal, you may realize that it's going to take considerably more work than you originally thought to achieve your dreams. Before you started, you didn't know that. Now you do. This is a very real consequence of Phase Five. Evaluation has the potential to tell you something you choose not to want to know. It gives you information, data and facts. Finding things you don't like in Phase Five is just as important as finding no flaws. Both outcomes allow you to determine what comes next. Your efforts get results.

Is This Going to Take Long?

How much time you spend inspecting your work depends upon a variety of factors. The most significant factor is the level of design-build project category. Level 1 Site Organization projects (taking a daily vitamin, cleaning out drawers, wearing a seatbelt) aren't all that complicated. They don't take that much time to complete, and they involve little or no risk. Such projects are frequently ongoing efforts. The greatest challenge is continuing what you've started. You can tell rather easily whether you've accomplished Site Organization projects, although the overall impact may not be as easily detected.

A higher level design-build project category brings greater complexity; hence, it will take longer to inspect. (You will need lots of batteries for your flashlight.) There's more to evaluate. Renovation or Rebuilding projects are by design complicated; they are intended to change your life significantly and thus affect many aspects of it. Other people may be affected by your decision to make your life more meaningful. You may spend time thinking about how your interaction with others has changed—a situation that you might not need to consider with a lower level project.

Keep in mind, however, that with higher level projects it's not other people's lives that you are inspecting. It's yours. Think twice before you begin conversations with those who have been part of your efforts: "Now that I've got my act together, have you ever thought about … ?" You are inspecting you in Phase Five—no one else. You are not judging others, and you are not judging yourself. The function of Phase Five is to evaluate. This term is without judgment and criticism. It means to observe and assess—to see things as they really are, not as you'd like them to be.

 **When you look at your life, what do you see and how do you feel about it?**

Another factor that influences how much time you will spend inspecting your work is your competency as an inspector. Do you know what's involved, how to proceed, what tools you'll need and the inspection criteria? Phase Five identifies what you will need to determine effectively the quality of what you've accomplished. You will need a few tools that you already have, and some new ones.

If you were doing a real home inspection, you would need things such as a magnet to determine the composition of pipes. You would need a marble to check how level the floors are, and a screwdriver to check for wood rot. A stepladder would help you get into an attic without pull-down stairs and explore rooms from different vantage points. An electrical tester would help you check circuit voltages. A clipboard, pencil and sheet on which to record your observations—and, of course, a flash-light—would all be needed to complete your inspection. But walking around your life requires a different set of tools.

Tack it Up

Inspection Tools

- Perspective
- Compassion
- Honesty
- Solitude

The tools listed above are necessary to complete Phase Five. If you can't put your hands on them, keep looking. It may take time to get everything you need.

By this point, the way you see your life should be different from when you began The Future Plan. You should feel more ownership of your own destiny. The manner in which you make decisions should be different. And, most important, the way you spend your time should reflect more of your priorities in life. You have purchased new tools and you have the statements to prove it—such as, "I'm worthy of change."

Perspective

The first tool needed for evaluation is perspective. This is the ability to put something into context. As you walk around your life, you will need a tool that allows you to compare and contrast. You will need a tool that allows you to understand how one change has had an impact on other aspects of your life. Perspective is the ability to step back and view your project from the outside looking in.

Compassion

Another essential tool is compassion. This is the ability to be unconditionally understanding. It is the exact opposite of being judgmental. While you were working on your projects, life was going on around you. Some of it was good. Some of it might have thrown you off

> Do you feel worthy of change?
>
> How do your actions represent how you wanted to spend your time when you started The Future Plan?
>
> How do your actions represent how you now want to spend your time?
>
> What has changed?
>
> What else has changed as a result of your project completion?
>
> What is the overall quality of your life now?

The Future Plan for a while. Then, when you decided to continue, you discovered that your stuff had been moved! Everything you had when you started wasn't there anymore. This is understandable. Give yourself a break; show yourself some compassion. Just start over. Consider your first, second or third attempts as practice.

A New Tool

For example, I remember lamenting to a good friend of mine the difficulty I was having with my children. I expressed how disappointed I was with myself. No matter what I did or said, my kids would do the exact opposite. Just when I thought I had parenting down to a science—BAM!—the kids changed right before my eyes.

My friend replied, "First of all, don't be so hard on yourself." Then, realizing this comment had no effect upon me, she said, "And second of all, it's not called 'parenting,' it's called 'practicing.'"

She had loaned me a tool.

Honesty

The third tool of evaluation is honesty. This is a tool that's often hidden somewhere ridiculous. You never know where it is, and you can spend hours, days and even months looking for it. You know you had it somewhere; in fact, you used it the other day. Where is it?

> *Evaluation has the potential to tell you something*
> *you choose not to want to know. It can also let you*
> *know that your choices have potential.*

Honesty is the ability to know the difference between reality and perception. As a tool, it allows you to be accurate in your self-evaluation. It puts an end to lies, cover-ups and excuses. Without this tool, your evaluation is pointless. You won't record any major damage because you'd have to do something about it. So you may pass up an opportunity to be truthful with yourself in exchange for being able to say, "I'm done." What you see, feel, hear, is exactly that—what you see, feel, hear. Being honest about what you've done—or not done—is essential to The Future Plan.

Solitude

The final tool of inspection is solitude. Construction is noisy. Home repairs are disruptive. Organizing your life can create a mess. At some point, however, you need the opportunity to be reflective, introspective, prayerful and quiet. You need solitude. This tool allows you to look at places not visible from the outside. You are essentially looking at the inside from the inside. By taking the time to be alone, peaceful and free from external stimulus, you can *be* the flashlight. Solitude allows you to think. It allows you to see what's behind this, around that, hidden up there or stuffed under something larger. This is the tool that says, "Stop! Be quiet."

To use this tool effectively, you will need to go off and be by yourself. Do what you need to do to make this happen. How long you will need to use the tool of solitude is a function of how many nooks and crannies are in your life. Borrowing someone else's solitude will not guarantee an uninterrupted source of introspection. You need your own. Let your passion continue to illuminate your soul.

That's it! Just four inspection tools will do it. Be sure you have them before you grab your clipboard and remove your carpenter's pencil from behind your ear. Now the only things you have to figure out are, "Where do I begin, what do I do next and what am I looking for?" This is not as hard—or as complicated—as it sounds. In fact, your life inspection is accomplished much as a real home inspection is. You will examine essentially the same five areas used during actual home inspections and in the same order. This allows you to be thorough. You won't be tricked into believing that something is fine if it's not.

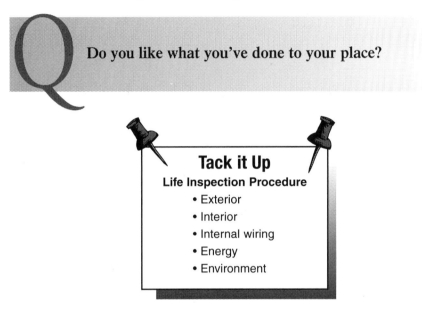

Q Do you like what you've done to your place?

Tack it Up
Life Inspection Procedure
- Exterior
- Interior
- Internal wiring
- Energy
- Environment

I'm told that home inspectors will closely examine roofs, exterior window casings, foundations, and so on before they walk inside. This is because it's easy to cover up water stains, interior water damage, rot, and a damp basement. If you see something suspicious on the exterior, you have reason to look more closely at the interior. The same goes for your life inspection. Phase Five begins with a look at what can be seen from the outside—before you look inside—as the following procedure suggests.

Exterior Inspection

Your exterior inspection looks at how different your life is as a result of completing your projects. It examines which actions, behaviors and practices are different from before. It looks at how your actions reflect your dreams and desires. Included in the exterior part of your life inspection is the concept of perspective.

> **Q** In what ways has what you've attempted to do changed the way you do other things—if at all?

"Everything looks fine from here."

Perspective is often something that happens over time. Therefore, you may have to wait until you have been actually pursuing your life-improvement goals—not just reading about them—before you can answer the following questions. To do otherwise would be equivalent to evaluating your fitness level after watching—not working out to—a workout video!

How has your dream life changed—if at all—since beginning your life-improvement efforts?

How would other people say your life has changed—if at all?

How does the current use of your time compare to how you'd rather be using your time?

What new projects—if any—seem to be needed now?

Interior Inspection

Your interior inspection looks at how you personally are different. This is the point where you go in through the front door and look around into your heart and soul. You explore what you are feeling about your efforts as well as how you have been changed. You look at your beliefs, attitudes and expectations. All the things you can't see or touch become what you are evaluating. It's often easier to identify an action than a feeling. You can say "Yes" or "No" to questions about action. But with emotions, thoughts and desires, it's more difficult.

How would you describe your self-esteem, self-identity and self-worth as a result of doing your project(s)?

How do you feel about your abilities to go out of your non-comfort zone?

What skills were most useful in doing your project(s)?

How do you feel about making additional changes to your life?

How has the source of your power (i.e., your internal motivators, passion, beliefs, etc.) affected the success of your projects(s)?

Internal Wiring

Phase Five asks you to look behind the surface at the systems and operations that make your life come alive. You often can't see the wiring behind walls. Sometimes you don't even know it's there unless something stops working. This is why it's also important to evaluate your electromechanicals and how they impact your future work.

"Electromechanicals" is not a term I had in my vocabulary until I started researching home inspections. How often in conversation does this term come up? Once? Twice? Never? To the homeowner, such things include wiring, plumbing, air conditioning, appliances and so on—systems and operations that make a structure come alive.

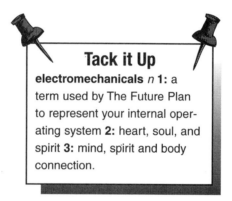

Tack it Up

electromechanicals *n* **1:** a term used by The Future Plan to represent your internal operating system **2:** heart, soul, and spirit **3:** mind, spirit and body connection.

In Phase Five, this term represents those aspects of your life that make you operate. It identifies your internal systems—your personal and spiritual health, fitness, safety habits and so on. It represents the connection between your mind, body and soul.

> How has your health been affected as a result of your project(s)?
>
> What behaviors related to your mind, spirit and body did you change as a direct or indirect outcome of your life-improvement efforts?
>
> How can you continue to enhance your mind, spirit and body?

Energy Considerations

Your next area of inspection involves energy considerations, which look at how efficiently you used your time and the source of your power. Phase Five uses the considerations of energy to help you evaluate the role that passion played—or didn't play—in your work.

It took many different kinds of energy from many different sources to get your projects planned and implemented. It is taking energy now to do your life (home) inspection. Although not all home inspections consider energy in their evaluations, The Future Plan encourages you to recognize the potential power passion has played in your decision-making, for it was from this energy source that you asked yourself, "So, what do you want to do?"

How effective were you at managing your time, resources and energy expenditures?

What did you learn about the role of passion in your life?

How else can passion serve as your guide in making future decisions?

What, if anything, do you need to do to pursue your passions more actively?

Why do you think you chose the projects you did?

&nvironmental Concerns

Environmental concerns looks at how people in your environment are responding—or not responding—to your life-improvement efforts. Not all of your friends, coworkers, family members and relatives will be supportive. Some may even try to sabotage your efforts. People around you may not know how to deal with the changes you have made in your life. By evaluating how others are responding or have been affected by your life-improvement efforts, you get valuable information. For instance, you may learn what you might want to do differently next time, who your friends really are, what approach was most effective, what communication skills you have and which ones you need and so on.

Being aware of the needs of others also helps to direct future projects. Taking the feelings of others into account is part of The Future Plan, just as recognizing that your decisions may affect people in different ways. You may have found yourself surprised, amazed, let down or uplifted by the reactions of those around you.

Q What impact did your life-improvement efforts have on others?

Who was most affected?

Who provided the most resources towards your efforts?

How would you change the manner in which you communicated with others during your work?

When making additional life improvements, what would you do differently with regard to the involvement of others?

Sharpen Your Carpenter's Pencil

It goes without saying that a carpenter's pencil is needed for the completion of Phase Five. You will also need time—even years. Although you can do this evaluation now (and access what you've changed in your life up to this point), you are encouraged to use a tool that can be erased, so you can continually evaluate your work. An "official" inspection sheet is provided in Appendix E, at the back of the book. This inspection worksheet is very thorough. It takes into account the many different kinds of projects you will try in the months ahead as well as those you've already started. It looks at the big picture by evaluating your entire life—not just one project.

Whether you did (or plan on doing) all of the exercises offered during the five phases, skipped a few or only scribbled in the margins, the fact that you took the time to look at ways to make your life more meaningful qualifies you for the final life inspection exercise. You have changed. Something in your life is different from when you began because time has passed. You can't help but change with the passage of time. For example, I hope you know more about motivation than when you started—at least that was the intent of *my* project.

Q How would you describe the overall condition of your life after making one or more life improvements?

What did you learn from The Future Plan?

How successful do you feel about your efforts?

What work still needs to be done?

That's it! All five phases of The Future Plan have been presented. Even though you may have to borrow someone else's flashlight to complete your work, you are well on your way. You have everything you need—except maybe a working flashlight. Despite banging it against a countertop, your flashlight isn't going to work unless *you* replace the batteries!

Hitting The Nail on The Head

- Phase Five is where you inspect your life.

- There are four tools that are required for doing a life inspection: honesty, solitude, contemplation and understanding.

- There is a systematic method to conducting your life inspection.

- The process of inspection progresses from exterior to interior to electromechanicals to energy consideration and concludes with environmental issues.

- Life inspections can reveal that there's more to be done or that your dream life has been achieved.

- Keep working flashlights around your life.

Houses Don't Paint Themselves

I always wanted to be somebody, but I should have been more specific.

—Lily Tomlin

N ow that you've worked through all five phases of The Future Plan, it's worth repeating that change only happens when you act. I speak from experience. You can wish your toilets to clean themselves, but until you physically go to the store, buy the cleaner, spray it on the toilet, let it bubble up and scrub it all off, your toilet won't get clean.

Although it would be great if you didn't have to do anything in order to get something, The Future Plan has made it clear that you can bring more happiness into your life if and when you act. When you finally make the connection between action attitude and change on a regular basis, you can have it all.

It is your perspective on life that greatly influences your ability to change. For instance, if you see the glass as always half-empty and you're not even sure you like what's left, you have a negative outlook on life. If you know it's going to be a bad day because your bagel has a hole in the middle, you have a bad attitude. The more you can free yourself from any degree of negativity, the more you allow yourself to be free — and the more you will change.

Low self-worth is often at the root of negativity. Unless you take the time to become good at being your own self-worth builder (see Chapter 7), you will have significant difficulty changing your life. You just won't feel worth the effort.

For example, if you view everything that happens around you as further evidence that you have no friends, hate your job, or that everyone is out to get you, you respond (consciously or unconsciously) accordingly. You eventually prove yourself to be right. But this is wrong. You deserve to live in your dream life. You can turn a negative attitude into one that will help you achieve your goal(s). You can do this because you have a brain. You can think, reason and do what it takes to build your self-worth.

A MATTER OF ATTITUDE

Directions: Next to each characteristic, place a T for TRUE or an F for FALSE to indicate if you assume that characteristic a majority of the time.

1. _____ I think about how to reach my goal(s).

2. _____ I point out the faults of others.

3. _____ I notice the faults of others on a regular basis.

4. _____ I think that every day is a new day.

5. _____ I marvel at other people's stupidity.

6. _____ I believe that I have potential.

7. _____ I dislike being asked "How are you?" because I know the person asking really doesn't care.

8. _____ I question why someone is being nice to me.

9. _____ I offer to help others on a regular basis.

10. _____ I frequently notice the qualities of others.

11. _____ I often wonder, "What's in this for me?"

12. _____ I know that when something breaks, it can usually be fixed.

13. _____ I take responsibility for my state of mind.

14. _____ I ask complete strangers "How are you?" then listen to what they say.

15. _____ I think others are waiting for me to fail so they can point it out to me.

16. _____ I would send flowers to myself if no one else was going to and I wanted them.

17. _____ I have no goals or dreams because they won't ever come true.

18. _____ I blame others for the way I get treated by them.

19. _____ I value every moment, second and day.

20. _____ I rarely laugh when I'm by myself.

21. _____ I live for 5 p.m., weekends and vacations.

22. _____ I think I have a high level of self-esteem.

23. _____ I see little meaning in what I do.

24. _____ I think motivational books like this one are pointless.

25. _____ I laugh at my own stupidity.

26. _____ I think about how motivational books like this one might make my life better.

Scoring. Circle each of the following statements that you marked F for FALSE: 2, 3, 5, 7, 8, 11, 15, 17, 18, 20, 21, 23, 24.

Circle each of the following that you marked T for TRUE: 1, 4, 6, 9, 10, 12, 13, 14, 16, 19, 22, 25, 26.

_____ Total Score = Total number of statements you circled above.

How do you approach life?

Through what kind of a lens do you look through at life—one that is positive, or one that is negative?

⊞alf Empty? Or Half Full?

The numbers in the row marked FALSE are negative indicators. This is why you are counting how many of these traits are not true so you can come up with one total positive attitude score. The numbers in the row marked TRUE are positive indicators. Using your Total Score, consider what this reveals about the kind of potential you have for change or how much you need to work on your attitude so you can change. When your attitude is negative, you need to make turning around your negativity into a project, create action items and deadlines, and get to work! True motivation comes from the inside out.

 **So how did you do?**

Interpreting Your Score

22–26 This score suggests a very upbeat and positive attitude about life in general. You enjoy people, and your perception of your environment reflects a high level of self-esteem. You have what it takes to make changes of any size because your attitude is a can-do one. Go for your dream life. You will achieve it.

14–21 This score suggests there's room for improvement. You are still relying on external sources of motivation to make yourself happy. Work on owning your own perceptions. Try not to see the glass as half-empty but focus (via thinking) on finding a water fountain. Don't be afraid to take care of yourself and treat yourself better. You can select projects of any size. Think about your approach. Know that this will be work and that it's your job to do your project(s) from start to finish. Keep cleaning the lens you use to view life by looking for the small pleasures and gifts. There is plenty of room for a more productive attitude. Look inward. Trust your potential.

0–13   This score suggests a significant amount of negativity in your perception of life. An adjustment of your attitude will need to be included as part of your planning process. Go back and make it a project if you want. Until you change the way you look at your environment, the glass will always be half-empty and change will not happen. It will take considerable thinking on your part to channel your actions. But, as I've previously pointed out, you have the tools to direct your outlook and to identify what you need to do to build your self-perception. Go back and focus on Chapter Four. And keep in mind that you're reading this book for a reason. You do care about you. Believe that change is possible. Believe that you can create your future. Believe in you.

> *They always say that time changes things, but you actually have to change them yourself.*
> —Andy Warhol

Getting Over It

If you are angry over what you just discovered, this suggests one more reason to adjust your attitude! It's difficult to admit having an unproductive (negative) attitude. It's hard to say that you don't care enough about yourself to want to create your future or that you rely on external motivation as opposed to passion to power your actions. But you have to admit such things so you can move on. Don't be afraid to use your intelligence to interpret the signals that are telling you it's time for an attitude adjustment.

The indicators, or characteristics, used to identify positive attitudes in the last exercise are "how to" examples for improving your attitude. Small alterations in your behavior will improve your attitude and, with small attitude improvements, will come more constructive behavior indicative of a positive attitude (i.e., what goes around, comes around).

For example, number 24 in the exercise raises the issue of reading motivational books. Hopefully, you marked that statement "false." The very act of reading *this* book will enhance your attitude, provide you with a strategy for self-improvement, inspire you to take care of yourself and so on. The more motivational books you read, the more you will be exposed to similar kinds of ideas. These ideas will become internal sources of motivation and provide you with a foundation for building a positive attitude. So, one way to enhance your attitude is to read more motivational books.

> *My philosophy is that not only are you responsible for your life, but doing the best at this moment puts you in the best place for the next moment.*
>
> —Oprah Winfrey

Another way to construct a more positive attitude is to start being more aware of who is in your environment and what kind of an outlook they possess. I believe that people assume either a negative or positive outlook on life as a function of their personality. You know people who are, on average, positive thinkers. You also know those who have a more negative filter. Which group do you spend most of your time with? Seek out positive people.

Odds are that you may know a group of people who qualify for the negative column because they all hang out together! Not only do they actually choose to see the glass as half-empty, but they talk endlessly about how long it will take before they all die from dehydration. Misery loves miserable company! Likewise, positive energy, positive people and positive attitudes are contagious.

One of the best ways to become more positive is to hang around positive people and observe their behaviors. What is it that they do? How do they treat you and others? What kind of a sense of self do they possess? Think about the most positive person you know. How does this person act on a daily basis? How does he or she view life's more diffi-cult moments? What kind of faith does this person possess? Now, think about you.

How would someone describe your attitude?

How do your attitudes and behaviors compare to someone who has a positive attitude? What are some of the more significant differences between you and this person? You can make generalizations about the cause-and-effect relationship between outlook on life and behavior. Positive people tend to focus on action, productivity and moving from one place to another. They ask "How?" to make their lives better. Positive people don't get caught up in the "What ifs?"

Positive people actively look for ways to improve existing relationships. They build relationships. They aren't possessive about their circle of friends. Those with more negative outlooks on life settle for the relationships they have already established. They settle for lower standards of respect or enjoyment from those relationships. As a result, many of their relationships are characterized by negative behaviors such as judging others, taking one another for granted, speaking poorly of one another and an unhealthy dependency. People with negative attitudes tend to drain or suck the energy right out of you. They bring you down.

Positive people are either working on accepting or have accepted that life isn't always fair. They look for the lessons in a tragedy. They explore ways of dealing with their emotions. They grow from life and move on. Negative people dwell on and in the past and waste valuable time feeling bad about what's already gone by. They often have unfinished business (unresolved issues or conflicts) that stay that way because they don't believe they can be resolved. They let these things interfere with their present lives and prevent a more meaningful future. Negative people prefer to hold onto baggage instead of letting go of it to make room for passion. Negative people don't rent dumpsters.

Positive people know that change is essential in life and adapt to it. Negative people cling to the misery they know and make it part of their daily existence. This helps to fuel their negativity. Stated in another way, one of the most significant differences between people with a positive and those with a negative attitude is that positive people take responsibility for their actions. Negative people play the victim and blame other people, places and things for their behaviors and negative outlook on life.

> *Boredom is not a state of mind. Boredom is the state of not using your mind.*

Because the kind of attitude you have determines the way in which you view your environment, consider the relationship between attitude and boredom. There is no such thing as the perfect job, perfect wife, perfect child, perfect car, etc. It's how you perceive your job, wife, child, car that determines how you feel about these things. Boredom is characteristic of people who have a negative attitude, since most of the things that make up their daily lives are boring to them. Even the word "boring" is a common part of their vocabulary: "What a boring movie." "She's just so boring." "My job bores me to death."

The reality is that negative people have chosen to interpret their surroundings this way and aren't doing much to change their outlook. They assume the "I'm bored" attitude in response to their perception, causing others to treat them as if they were bored—or boring. The cycle is perpetuated.

Positive people find ways to see their environment in a manner that is not dull, draining or boring. They find ways to interpret what's going on around them in a manner consistent with a love of life and a positive self-perspective. Every minute is valued; they don't have time to waste. Central to taking the boredom out of your life is getting back in touch with how you want to be spending your time.

In Search of Contentment

Small actions can lead to larger actions. When you desire to do something big, you can prepare by getting your life organized, re-arranging your priorities, and by adding or deleting things to your life. This may take you longer, but it also may enhance your success at starting something from the ground up. This is an important point to make. Take it one step at a time. You don't have to take it fast. Experience success and failure. Get good at taking risks, then take it higher. The story that follows demonstrates how this process is put into practice.

One evening, a man arrived home from work exhausted. Apparently he had not had a good day, and his family could sense this. When he saw his wife, he said, "My life stinks. All I do is get up, go to work and come home. For what?"

She asked him, "So, what do you want to do?"

He barked a response at her. "First, I don't know. Second, I wouldn't have time to do it if I did know! Third, you probably wouldn't let me anyway."

The women repeated her question. There was no response.

A couple of weeks later, the man arrived home later than usual with large packages under each arm. He said to his wife, "Well, you told me I should pursue my dreams and do things I've always wanted to do." He asked his kids to put the packages on the table. As if reading their minds, he said, "You're probably wondering what I bought. Here, I'll show you."

Home-brew paraphernalia was emptied piece by piece onto the table. "Beer?" asked his wife. "Can we help?' asked his children. Shortly thereafter, the father and his two children (i.e., his assistant brew masters) measured and poured the right amount of hops into big bins. The mother observed from a distance with one hand holding her nose, the other over her eyes.

After work, the father and his kids worked on their project. They read about different grains, visited home breweries, and made labels for their product. That Christmas, it was home brew for everybody— complete with a big red bow on the jug handles.

But by New Year's the thrill of home brewing had diminished. "I have an idea. Does anyone want to hear it?" the man asked, then sighed. "It probably can't happen anyway, so what's the point in telling you about it?"

"Does it have to do with beer?" asked his son.

"No," the father said as he shook his head. "I just thought it would be fun to be on a ski racing team this winter."

For the next eight weeks, the father flew in the door every Wednesday night after work, raced upstairs to grab his gear, raced back through the kitchen, then raced out the door to go downhill ski racing. And every Wednesday night—as promised—the father woke up his former assistant brew masters and showed them that evening's medal—given out to all participants.

As February approached, the home brewer turned ski racer announced that he had another idea. It began, "You probably won't let me, but ..." followed by a request to play basketball on a local team once a week.

"Why are you asking me?" replied his wife.

"Does everyone get a medal there, too?" asked his son.

The increase in the man's apparent happiness was encouraging to his wife. But she knew he still wasn't pursuing his true passion in life. Then, one evening, her husband took his wife aside and asked, "Wouldn't it be nice to own our own sailboat?"

"Finally!" she responded with a smile.

That spring, his children watched their father run in the door after work. This time, however, he carried sailing magazines, faxes, and newspapers. He made phone calls, e-mailed boat brokers, and set up appointments. He talked sailing. For weeks, his family listened with interest to the differences between a head and a hull and why the boat was a she not an it. By April, he had purchased his first sailboat.

"Do you have a name for it?" asked his daughter.

"Her. A name for her," corrected the father.

"Whatever," she commented.

The man slowly removed a list of names from his suit pocket. The home brewer turned ski racer turned basketball player turned sailboat owner said, "The most special times of my life were spent sailing with my Dad—your grandfather. We thought we would sail around the world together." He paused, then said in a quieter voice, "But, then he died. I was only twenty. We never got the chance."

The children looked at their father with sadness in their eyes. Then the daughter asked, "Do you have a name for it—I mean her?"

The son of a sailor smiled at his wife. She returned his smile, for she knew that he was finally beginning to pursue his passion.

Softly he replied, "*Legacy.* I think I'll call her *Legacy.*"

My How You've Changed!

By doing The Future Plan, you learn how to change internally. Regardless of the scope of the job you complete, you are different because of the process of change. In fact, you will never be the same again. You have done (or will do) something to take back control of your destiny and bring more enjoyment into your life. This will leave you feeling a sense of accomplishment and satisfaction. It will also leave you more perceptive about your potential.

The more you change, the better you get at it. Less effort is needed to jump the obstacles and more value is seen in the changing process. The connection between a positive attitude, your williningness to take action and change is automatic.

Just because you want to build a barn in your backyard doesn't mean that your half-acre lot will double in size. Hoping that your boss will take early retirement doesn't mean that your job satisfaction will improve. Although it would be convenient to wish change into happening, change will only happen when you act. Change is a function of your emotions and how they get channeled. Your ability to think and feel is the foundation for change. Your attitude matters because houses don't build themselves.

Hitting the Nail on the Head

\ A positive attitude will move you forward.

\ Changing your behaviors is one way to change your attitudes.

\ Low self-worth and an inability to change are connected.

\ A negative attitude causes—not only you, but others—to block your change efforts.

\ You can change your attitude.

\ Boredom is a result of a negative attitude.

\ Practice at changing.

The Tools of Transition

By the time I catch up to what's in style, it goes out of style. My new approach is just to be patient, to wait. Eventually the very first end table I ever bought will be the latest interior designer's antique dream. Although somehow I doubt that; it's just old. Ugly, too. Come to think of it, I don't think I liked it when I bought it at a yard sale, but it was all I could afford at the time. Still, I hold onto it, letting it take up valuable space in my basement. It is a reminder of where I began, not where I am. Maybe that's why I keep it.

Think about your life five years ago. Think about your physical health, your outlook on life, what you were doing to be productive, and the people, places, and things that brought you enjoyment. Try to remember who, if anyone, was dependent upon you—and you on them. Consider the challenges you faced back then, whom you admired and your faith. Now, review those same issues in your mind as they currently exist.

You can't deny that something has changed—if nothing else, you are older. You probably made a few good and a few bad choices in the past five years. I recently asked a group of young adults how many times they have experienced the date being all the same number (2/2/22, 3/3/33, 4/4/44, 5/5/55, 6/6/66, 7/7/77, 8/8/88, 9/9/99). When they came up with only one date, I knew I had made a bad decision by asking the question. But it does point out that time is always giving us the chance to change.

You are a product of change. You've been changing since you were born. Whether you believe it or not, you're more prepared to create change in your future than you might think. Change is the one inescapable aspect of life that will keep occurring whether you want it to

Q What has remained the same and what is different in your life five years ago and now?

or not. Remember the eight-track cassette player? Drinking water straight out of your faucet? Being out of cash? Not being able to get someone on the phone? These are examples of the future becoming the past.

The Future Plan encourages you to be the change initiator. It inspires you to create something new in response to your desire to live a more meaningful life. Consider the fact of life that change is your goal. If you can adapt, you will survive.

There are four essential skills needed to work with change. Without these, you may find it more difficult to complete your projects using your punch lists (Appendix D). Each skill enables you to put your energy where it will have the greatest impact. Instead of spinning your wheels, you will be more intentional in your behavior. I call these four skills the "tools of transition."

Life's toolbox has plenty of nuts.

Tack it Up

Tools of Transition
(Skills of Change)
- Creativity
- Time Management
- Communication Skills
- Controlling Fears

Creativity

The first tool of transition is creativity. As you've already experienced, the ability to envision, dream and imagine a different life allows you to see what it is you are trying to create. Just because you don't think you have what it takes to be more creative doesn't make it true. In fact, research shows that it is your belief that you are creative that separates you from those who are not creative! (For more information, read *Jump Start Your Brain* by Doug Hall.)

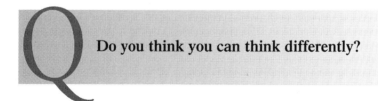

Do you think you can think differently?

Creativity is a mind thing. The best way to get your creative thought flowing is to stimulate your mind. Don't just sit and stare into space. Get up. Explore what other people have already envisioned, dreamed, created and imagined.

The first place I go when I'm inspired to be creative—to remodel my kitchen, for instance—is to the bookstore. Here I can find magazines and books on kitchen designs. The next place I go is to a "do-it-yourself" store; I walk up and down the aisles of faucets, sinks and tiles, gathering ideas. Because imagination requires many different kinds of stimuli, I also check out the kitchens in every home I visit. (Be forewarned.)

To get more creative ideas, ask, "Where can I stimulate my mind?" Take a moment to consider what you can do to generate brain activity. Talk a walk. Go to the grocery store. Sit on a playground and watch the kids. Read a magazine.

> *Imagination is more important than knowledge.*
> —Albert Einstein

Another effective way to stimulate your brain is to engage continuously in dialogues. Seek out people who appeal to you and find out why. As was previously suggested, get into conversations with strangers. Talk, talk, talk. The exercise of making your brain organize your thoughts so others can understand them gets your thought process working harder. Solicit the opinion of others by asking, "Have you ever heard about anyone who … ?" Again, place yourself in environments that help you generate new ways of thinking.

Go for quantity when trying to stimulate ideas. The volume of ideas you generate and surround yourself with helps create better ideas. Make lists. Collect pictures and lots of other visual stimuli. The result will be more design-build project ideas with more ways to achieve them.

Finally, remember that your brain is connected to the rest of your body. Generating ideas is more productive when you are rested, relaxed and in a good mood. Go for a run. Take a nap. Watch a Three Stooges movie. You can intentionally make yourself think more creatively by laughing because laughter helps you become more rested, relaxed and in a good mood. Put thought into the kinds of stimuli that will amuse you. It might be a person, place or thing. Try to "crack yourself up" when no one else is looking.

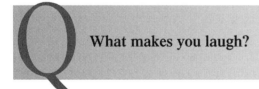

Q What makes you laugh?

> *The less one has to do, the less time one finds to do it in.*
>
> —Lord Chesterfield

Time Management

The next helpful tool of transition is time management. Just because we get twenty-four hours in a day doesn't mean we know how to use those hours efficiently. Think about the last time you had someone do work in your home. When you pay an hourly rate, the productivity in each hour matters. The same standard needs to apply to your life. Even though you aren't literally paying yourself for every hour you work on your life, you should produce as if you were doing just that!

The first skill of effective time management is the ability to set priorities. In Phase Two you became familiar with the importance of priority setting. You were asked to consider the question, "What is the most important thing to you?" then to consider the next most important thing, and so on. You learned that this is how priorities are established.

Priorities are also established by what makes common sense. For example, knowing that a primer needs to go on your wall before a light color of paint prevents your having to put on three and four coats to cover the old color. Knowing that redoing your floors means sawdust all over your house tells you to paint *after* the floors are done and the dust vacuumed up. If you don't think about priority order for your projects before you begin them, you might find yourself moving backwards, not forwards. By setting priorities, you can manage your time more effectively.

Another time management skill is to take shortcuts. Don't believe that there is only one way to proceed. Look for ways to eliminate time-consuming activities if they aren't really necessary. One way to do this is to learn from others. Ask people how they did what they did, or got to where they are in life. Listen to their stories. You could spend years in school, for instance, only to learn that not everyone who is doing what you want to do has that particular degree! Look for the most direct way to achieve your life-improvement goal without jeopardizing its structural integrity.

Tack it Up

Caution! Hard Hat Required!

Be moral, ethical and fair in how you go about achieving your goals. Taking a short-cut or two doesn't mean selling someone short. Using substandard building materials is replacing quality—and safety—in exchange for price and convenience. You will be the ultimate judge of what qualifies as a shortcut and what is just plain wrong.

Planning ahead is another way to enhance your time management skills. It's amazing how much stuff you can get done if you plan your day. When you follow a schedule or routine, for instance, you tend to make better use of your time. Remember the saying, "If you want something done, ask a busy person?" Being busy forces you to get organized. In Phase Four, the role of punch lists was introduced as a means of taking action to achieve change. Making more time in which to accomplish your action items can be done in the same way. Simply apply the same concepts to your everyday life. Every morning, write a "to do" list. Every night, check off what you've accomplished!

> *I must govern the clock, not be governed by it.*
> —Golda Meir

Finally, you will have to make room for your passion pursuit. This means freeing up time and knowing how you spend your time. Use a daily planner to chart where your time is going. Study an entire week or month. You may be surprised to discover that you watch four hours of television per day (as does the average American). What would happen if you turned off your set and turned on your efforts to achieve your dream life? Go through your week and delete those things from your "to

What do you do that someone else could do instead?

do" list that take time but do not move you toward your life-improvement goal. You can also transfer obligations or time-consuming tasks to someone else.

Communication Skills

The third tool of transition involves having effective communication skills. As passion is to power, communication skills are to change. Being able to express yourself effectively is the key to developing and implementing your work. Without effective communication skills, your ability to ask for what you need accurately and clearly is harder than it has to be. In fact, you may never initiate change if it involves other people because of your unwillingness to express yourself. And you will need other people—at one point or another—to accomplish your life-improvement goal.

You have been communicating all your life—at times clearly and, at other times, ineffectively—and have developed a particular method of interacting with others. These communication patterns were learned. This means they can be unlearned and replaced with more productive ones. Skills that reflect a high level of self-worth and the desire to protect yourself are required for good communication.

How effective are you at communicating your needs?

Whether you are actively seeking the advice of others, informing those who may be affected by your actions of your plans, inquiring about various services or resources, soliciting support from significant others, questioning those who appear to be blocking your efforts, challenging false assumptions and intentions, protecting your rights, or simply expressing your needs, how well you do it will affect the outcome. Here are a few tips that can open the doors to the process of change and assist you throughout The Future Plan.

Tips for Enhanced Communication

Tip 1: **Speak clearly and directly.** You wouldn't instruct someone renovating your house to "Just do whatever." Yet, when someone is kind enough to ask, "What do you want me to do?" or "What are you trying to tell me?" the natural response is to beat around the bush. The more specific and direct you can be when asking for what you want, the greater the chance that you will be heard and accurately understood.

Example: *If you want to change your job, you can communicate your desire by saying, "I need to get another job. I am not challenged, and I feel under-appreciated."*

Tip 2: **Use specific action words.** The key to change is action. By using specific actions words (verbs) in action sentences (what it is you want), you give the receiver something to understand and respond to.

Example: *"I need to get another job. I am not challenged, and I feel under-appreciated. Do you know anyone who is looking for someone with my skills?"*

Tip 3: **Set a reference time.** The key to action is a deadline. When expressing your needs, let the receiver know your time frame. If you leave this information out of your communication, the receiver can't register your request as a specific request for action. But if you state a specific time or date and refrain from saying "someday" or "in the near future," both the sender (that's you) and the receiver have more substantial information upon which to build.

Example: *"I need to get another job. I am not challenged, and I feel under-appreciated. Do you know anyone who is looking for someone with my skills? I want to be in a different position by May 1 of this year."*

Tip 4: **Leave the door open.** The key to reaching a deadline is resourcefulness. The process of change involves making decisions based upon your personal circumstances, which include the availability and nature of your resources. These are not just financial resources, as you'll discover in a later chapter. The resources needed to improve your life often have nothing to do with monetary worth.

Your ability to take something away from every dialogue you have is a skill successful people use on a regular basis. Every interaction gets turned into a possibility of some kind. Every communication becomes a future contact. Every chance encounter becomes an opportunity to network. As you talk about your plans, share your needs, seek support and solicit information (to name a few purposes of communication), consider the value in prolonging the conversation.

Specifically, ask yourself before the communication is over, "What can I take away from this encounter?" Often the answer will be to ask for a business card or phone number, follow up with a note, take the person up on an offer, stop by or drop in, leave your number, ask to let you know if they hear of anything, and follow up with a phone call. When you leave the door open on a regular basis, it's amazing how action plans come to life.

Example: *"I need to get another job. I am not challenged, and I feel under-appreciated. Do you know anyone who is looking for someone with my skills? I want to be in a different position by May 1 of this year. If you think of anyone, please call me at this number and, if it's okay, I'd like to call you in a few weeks."*

Tip 5: **Use matching nonverbal communication.** Eighty percent of all communication is body language, or nonverbal communication. It's often not what you say, but what you do that speaks the loudest. Think about how your body posturing matches your words. Avoid the extremes of looking weak or being aggressive.

Being aggressive is what is perceived if you point, stand too close or put your hands on your hips. Stand tall (or sit tall). Don't cross your arms or your legs. Maintain eye contact. Avoid getting behind tables or chairs while talking with someone (this can be perceived as a protective blocking mechanism).

The best way to determine how your body language communicates when you talk is to look in the mirror. Observe assertive body language in others. Practice it in front of a mirror or with a friend.

> *Far better it is to dare mighty things, to win glorious triumphs even though checkered by failure, than to rank with those poor spirits who neither enjoy nor suffer much because they live in the gray twilight that knows neither victory nor defeat.*
>
> —Theodore Roosevelt

Controlling Fears

The final tool of transition centers on your ability to control your fears. One of the greatest obstacles to change is the four-letter word "fear." In order to embrace the change process, you need to understand the complexity of this simple term. Fear is an essential survival tool intended to warn of danger so you can "fight or take flight."

When you fail to identify, acknowledge and accept the fears that accompany the change process, you hold yourself back. All change comes with risk. It's part of the process, so assuming that you don't have anything to be afraid of isn't realistic. There's plenty of change that will leave you uncomfortable, anxious, nervous, resistant or doubtful. Here are some of the more common fears associated with making life improvements.

Which fear(s) do you use?

Fear of the unknown You fear the unknown out of natural instinct. The important point, however, is that you have intelligence and the ability to determine the difference between a rational and an irrational fear. Accept the fact that you may feel some level of fear, be okay with some degree of anxiety and then proceed.

I've never met anyone who made changes and didn't have doubts of some kind. Even after great things had happened as a result of their efforts, they still questioned and wondered, "What if..." A degree of self-doubt goes with the territory. Just keep it in perspective, and take the time you need to decide which fears are real and require your attention and which are irrational.

Fear of failure The most common fear is being afraid your efforts won't pay off. As I've said many times, just the effort you make to improve your life makes you successful. The outcome is a byproduct of that initial success. When facing this fear, ask yourself the most common fear-busting question, "What's the worst thing that will happen if I don't succeed?" Failure is an important part of life. How would you know what it meant to succeed without failure?

Fear of success Believe it or not, the fear of being successful can also prevent you from taking action that will lead to change in your life. If you do what you set out to do, will you be able to handle the pressure of sustaining that success? This is a rational question. What others think, though, can't be the criteria by which you judge your success. Again, look at the outcome of your efforts as the byproduct of your hard work. A position, title, paycheck or other modes of recognition won't make you successful—it's who you are from the inside out.

Fear of the opinions of others When you make a lot of noise during a home improvement project, others will notice. (Especially if you make a big mess, too.) Think about what happens when that twenty-square-yard dumpster arrives at your home. You are saying to the world, "Look, I'm going to do something." Then, you feel obligated/pressured to do something; you fear not being able to fill your dumpster.

Instead, focus on setting your own realistic expectations that are obtainable. The Future Plan asks you to explore those things that need to be considered before starting your projects and asks you to select a project or two that you can achieve. Why order a twenty-square-yard dumpster when you could really use a five-yard one? Set realistic goals, focus and proceed one step at a time.

Avoid giving control of your life to the expectations of someone else. It is natural, and even admirable, to want to please others and to make their lives better because of your efforts. But this isn't an issue of fear; it's an issue of maturity. Be sure to double-check your motives along the way.

Fear of self-discovery The one thing the process of change will do is make things inside of you different. That's the point. Yet this may not always feel comfortable. Maybe you don't want to know what lies under the twelve layers of wallpaper inside you—or even learn that there are twelve layers in the first place. Maybe your life has been adequate up to this point; why risk discovering your inadequacies, falsehoods, repressed fears, inability to deal with life or that someone you care about has really not been holding you back?

But life is not about just letting time pass. It is day after day of self-discovery. If pain, temporary misery, discomfort, anger or other emotions associated with change present themselves during the pursuit of your passions, you are making progress. The only thing to worry about is whether or not your dumpster is going to be large enough for your needs!

Fear of your own limitations The skills previously mentioned are learned and needed as you progress through The Future Plan. You may not know what you need to know until you realize you don't know it. Give yourself a break! For instance, it may only be when you are knee-deep in cement that you realize you should have worn those big ugly boots so you can get out.

Fear of the limitations of others People are dependent upon you as you currently exist. But you are about to change. What happens if they don't like the new you or they aren't as excited about your pursuit of happiness? What if they can't handle your happiness or newly discovered passions? They may just be trying to adjust and adapt to your different set of attitudes and behaviors. They may or may not have the skills to do this; they may or may not have the inspiration to do this.

For these reasons, it is important to bring these folks along with you early in the planning stages—to let them know what you have in mind, to share your ideas and to give them the opportunity to understand. You can prevent the potential fallout of not including them in your change process—jealousy, envy, anger, resentment, judgment, disappointment, self-doubt and the like. Behavior that results from such emotions not pleasant and can often have negative consequences. So, before you blame others, consider what role the changes you made, are making, or intend to make may play in triggering their reactions.

Remember, however, that your life-improvement efforts are not about the inadequacies of others. Use your communication skills to talk with those who matter in your life. Consider that maybe they would like to work alongside you or even help to hold your ladder.

Fear of change There's not much you can do about this last fear other than accept that it's real. This acceptance comes from understanding the process and nature of change. Yet even this knowledge rarely eliminates some degree of fear. Think of the fear of change more as being in a state of anticipation. If you've ever said, "I can't wait to see what this will look like when it's all done," then you've admitted your fear of change. What you really meant was, "I really hope I like how this turns out after all of this trouble."

> *Every man has the right to risk his own life—in order to save it.*
>
> —Jean Jacques Rousseau

"What if I run out of paint?"

If you were to examine each of these fears as its own can of paint, would you be running out to your local do-it-yourself home improvement store to return a few cans, or would you be stocking up on a particular color of fear just in case you think you might run out?

Remember, change is a natural force of nature. Fear is a natural reaction. Knowing more about what might prevent you from moving forward allows you to move forward. It will help you make choices that will lead to action that will lead to change. The end result will be what you want.

JOT IT DOWN

Directions: Make a list of your fears about making life
improvements in the spaces below.

_____

_____

_____

_____

_____

Change is good

Change will teach you things you don't know and challenge you to grow. Another significant benefit of change is the opportunity it gives you to learn new skills, challenge existing skills and expand your knowledge. You get to practice new communication skills, become more creative, learn how to use your time more effectively and handle your fears.

There are many other benefits of change. Because of change, you're able to think ahead or prepare for the inevitable—whether by intention or accident. It takes the pressure off of having to be certain about anything or having to explain why you are a different person today from who you were five years ago.

The very process of being an active participant in the planning and implementation phases of The Future Plan will bring you a renewed sense of personal worth. It makes you feel alive. How can you not find pleasure in that which you have created? By doing something—anything—to be more alive demonstrates the fact that you value the time you have on this planet. Your actions are a product of this joy.

Hitting The Nail on The Head

- Change is a natural force of nature.

- Change happens with time; it is a constant.

- You can improve your life with change, but you can't control the actions and perceptions of others.

- Creativity, time management, communication skills and controlling fears are four of the most significant skills needed for getting the job done.

- Structural integrity can't be compromised in the planning and implementation phases of your projects.

- Fear is a natural part of the change process.

15

Untapped Resources

I was never one to hide an empty coffee can in the back of a kitchen cupboard, filled with money for a rainy day. Not only does this money end up smelling like roasted coffee beans, it seems deceptive—it gives the impression you are trying to hide a dollar or two. No, I was never one to use an empty coffee can. I used my jewelry box.

After all, how great it is to have a place to keep discretionary dollars—totally unmarked bills that can't be traced! The fact that this fund never gets larger than five dollars is totally beside the point. The fact that everyone in the house knows where to find a couple of dollars whenever they need it is also totally beside the point. Whenever I reach into my jewelry box, I am reminded of the fact that there is always somewhere I can go to find something of value. I am never broke. I am never without resources.

As I have suggested, you are never without resources, either. Believe it or not, you're much wealthier than you think. You, too, have a coffee can of reserves, or a place where you can find the resources you need to accomplish your goals and complete your projects. There are probably hundreds of untapped resources at your disposal.

When selecting which project to start in Phase Four, don't limit your selection because of the potential financial expense. Give yourself more credit! Tap into all of your resources before claiming that you can't afford to do what you want. It's very possible that what you'll find is that you can't afford *not* to do it. Not having enough money or assuming you can't possibly afford to make changes in your life is taking the easy way out.

There's no need to go searching through cupboards or under mattresses for hidden funds. A dozen resources worth tapping are offered in this chapter and the next. Real dollars are only one of your potential stashes. These resources can be combined with other resources. You are the best one to discover your hidden talents, untapped resources and forgotten assets.

And remember the rule that applies in situations like this: Finders keepers!

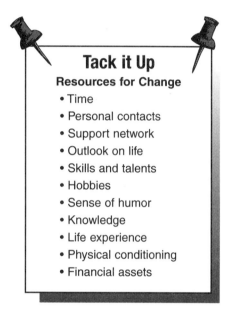

Tack it Up

Resources for Change
- Time
- Personal contacts
- Support network
- Outlook on life
- Skills and talents
- Hobbies
- Sense of humor
- Knowledge
- Life experience
- Physical conditioning
- Financial assets

Time

The first of twelve untapped resources for your consideration is the most important—time. If you don't spend time planning, selecting and carrying out your life-improvement projects, you will have wasted your time reading this book. It's worth repeating that houses don't paint themselves. Change won't happen unless you take the time to pick out the paint, figure out how you're going to pay for it and then don your overalls. Stop and spend time on you. Start now. You have the time.

Remember, the most basic tip in time management is setting priorities. The more time you can devote to the pursuit of your dream life, the sooner it will start to become a reality. Take the time to find more time in your day. Choose you first. Do what you need to do to get organized

*Things that matter most must never be at the mercy
of things which matter least.*
—Goethe

and prepared for change. You are given 24 hours a day, 168 hours a week, and 8,736 hours a year. Ask yourself, "What do I need to do to give myself some time?" Then do it.

Personal Contacts

There is truth in the saying, "It's not what you know that counts. It's who you know." Many of your project ideas will require someone else to open a door or two for you. Don't assume that you don't know anyone. In fact, you may not be aware of someone you know who knows someone else who can help you move closer to your goals. The only way to find this person is to stop and think—and talk to people. Take a look at the following list of questions that will spark your memory. It might be helpful to write the answers to these questions in a place where you can get to them when you need them. (Maybe your responses need to become part of your "to do" lists in Appendix D.)

Q Who do I know (or am related to) who is doing something similar to my life-improvement goal?

Who do I know who would hire me—even if it's just to give me a start?

Where could I go to get the names of employees in [company] to see if I know any of them or know of someone who might know one of them?

Who should I call, even if I don't know them?

Who do I know who has information useful to my work at hand?

The worst thing anyone can say to your request for help is "No." The worst answer to your question is "I don't know." When thinking about your personal contacts, don't think narrowly. Broaden your contact base. Include anyone and everyone with whom you've come in contact in your past—from your hometown dentist to the sister of a friend you met while on vacation. Consider who you interact with on a daily basis. Don't be too quick to cross someone off your list until you've explored all the various ways they might be able to assist you.

Consider relatives and the spouses of relatives and their relatives! Get out your high school yearbook (gag!). If you attended college, spend some time thinking about who might be a useful contact there. Contact the alumni office for names of graduates who might be willing to help because you attended their alma mater. When I travel, I'm amazed at how quickly travelers introduce themselves, give out business cards and inquire what I do for a living. At first I found this to be extremely flattering. Then I realized it wasn't me—everyone gets a card.

Your potential list of personal contacts is limitless. Who can bring you closer to your dream life? If you don't know anyone, find out who you need to know—and then get to know them.

Support Network

Recognizing the difference between your actual support network and your perceived support network is like recognizing the difference between having money in the bank and thinking you have money in the bank. In either case, you'll never know how much you've got until you need it all!

Your support network can consist of your immediate and extended family, your professional associates and even people you hire to serve in a support role. For example, a tutor, psychologist, marriage counselor, physical trainer, nutritionist or professor can be of great comfort and guidance to you. Although you usually have to pay for their services, it's often worth it.

There are those whose guidance and support are free (husbands, wives, children, parents, boss) as a result of their relationship to you. When considering the wealth of your support network, be realistic. Just because you expect someone to be part of your support network doesn't mean that they will be.

> *The better part of one's life consists of his friendships.*
>
> —Abraham Lincoln

You may have to expand your network. Look for the places in which you do have support and then build from there. Time used to foster healthy friendships can be time well-invested! There are many different kinds of friendships and many different kinds of friends. There are friends who have little time of their own to offer, but who would provide you with a few encouraging words over the phone. There are friends you can trust with your house key and things about yourself that you wouldn't tell anyone else.

The thing about the potential value in friendships is that you have to be willing to trust what's in reserve—what's already in the bank. You may not know just how supportive a friend can be until you ask for their support.

To free up some of your time to begin work on your project, consider which of your friends might be a valuable resource. What help do you need and who can help you? What can you offer in return? Take time to continue fostering friendships with all kinds of different people in your life. Be careful, however, about hanging around only with coworkers. If you see these people all day at work, eat lunch with them and play golf with them on weekends, it might be time to expand your horizons.

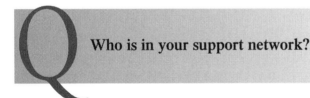

Q **Who is in your support network?**

At first it's okay not to have a lot of people whom you consider to be part of your support network. However, this list will have to grow in order for you to achieve higher level projects. Quality often goes further than quantity when it comes to relationships. What matters is how much support you feel you have from the people in your life now, versus how much support you'll need to accomplish your life-improvement goal.

Outlook on Life

The only person who can determine the value of your outlook on life is you. What do you see when you look around you? How do you feel about your potential? This vision will either be one of your largest assets or a major weight holding you back. Although the topic of attitude has been discussed in some detail, it's worth repeating that "Attitude is everything!" If you continually work on not seeing the glass as half-empty or as half-full, but focus instead on finding a water fountain, you will have all the wealth you need to afford your dream life.

As a reminder, keep your mind focused on questions such as "How do I change my life?" and "What do I need to do today to move closer to my dream life?" Stay away from such limiting questions as "Will I ever live where I want?" and "What else could get in my way?"

Skills and Talents

In many ways, the design-build project category you choose speaks to your perception of your current and potential skills and talents. It also highlights the skills you may need to improve upon. This is what makes life so exciting. It makes you engage your many abilities and take them higher and higher or wider and wider. You often don't know what you are actually capable of achieving until you test your limits.

A talent can be anything that sets you apart from others. A high degree of intelligence is a talent. The ability to talk to teenagers is a talent. Knowing how to console people is a talent. Caring for the elderly is a talent. Bringing world leaders together in the name of peace is a talent. Fixing cars is a talent. Tiling your kitchen floor is a talent. Catering a Christmas party is a talent. Operating a dance studio is a talent. Raising wonderful children is a talent.

Talent is also how you perceive your abilities. To achieve your dream life, you will need to get intimate with your talents. What are you good at? What do you do better than most other people? What do you do that other people don't—or won't—do? The more you recognize the many gifts within you, the more powerful they become.

The better you think you are at something—with few exceptions—the better you become.

Higher level design-build project ideas will likely involve building and expanding your current skills and talents. Higher level design-build project ideas will almost always involve learning a few new things, too. Your lower level project ideas can be accomplished with your current capabilities. But don't limit your project selection because you don't think you have what it takes. Remember, you can always return to Appendix C to add to or change your project selections.

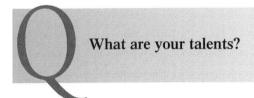

What are your talents?

You now have an opportunity to explore your skill and talent inventory found in Appendix F, "Self-Assessment Inventory." Keep in mind that this is your perception of your abilities and not what others may think—or what is actually the case. When you identify a particular skill area that needs some work, there's no one but you who gets to decide if the work will get done or not. Remember, it's your life. Your choice. Your future.

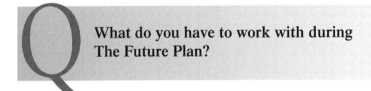

What do you have to work with during The Future Plan?

Likewise, it is important to acknowledge those skill areas you feel you have mastered. These become tools that you can count on—some of which might also be used to sharpen the less-mastered skills. Recognizing your strengths is one way to enhance your confidence. As stated many times throughout this book, your self-worth needs to be high in order to pursue your passions. Go ahead and admit what you know how to do and what you don't know how to do.

Caution! Your level of self-worth at the time you take the Self-Assessment Inventory will affect your responses and their accuracy. However, if you ask yourself, "On a regular basis, do I [fill in the skill item]?" you can get a valid look at your skills. This information is useful. Take a moment and assess your skills.

ccepting the Data

If you discover that you need to build your skills, put that on your "to do" list. Don't let the fact that you aren't up on the most recent computer software prevent you from changing jobs. Take an evening course to be up-to-date on the latest software. Don't let the fact that you don't know how to speak a foreign language prevent you from traveling abroad. Borrow foreign language learning tapes from your local library, take a language immersion class or hire a tutor. You are the only one drawing the line that determines where your competencies begin and end.

> **Do you have what you need to make your life more meaningful?**

Resources are everywhere. We've only discussed five so far. The next chapter lists the remaining items. Now you know where to look. But what about that hidden stash? Somewhere in your life, you have a stash of valuable resources. Try looking in places you've never thought about before, and of course look in the back of your kitchen cupboards. If you can't find an empty coffee can with lots of loose change, go into the freezer and unwrap anything that looks suspicious. If you sense that you are being watched, keep looking. Plant a decoy. Keep the mystery alive. Then find what you've been looking for in the mirror.

Hitting The Nail on The Head

- You have a greater wealth of resources than you may think.

- Spend time identifying who can help you achieve your goal.

- What you know is not as important as your ability to learn.

- Talent is in the eye of the beholder.

16

Gee, You've Got Potential

> *Birds sing after a storm; why shouldn't people feel as free to delight in whatever remains to them?*
> —Rose Kennedy

W hen people ask me, "What's the difference between a good and a bad speaker?" I reply, "How good or bad they think they are." This is a conclusion I have reached as a result of many years as a public speaker. Now, ask me the difference between a good and a bad plumber, and I would respond with a completely different answer: ranging from how highly they thought of their skills or how much they charged to whether they kept their promises to show up on time and get the job done right.

There is a connection to be found between *your* perception of *your* abilities and the amount of effort you are willing to exert to accomplish your life-improvement goal. Confidence is an internal motivator. Belief in your potential to achieve your goals in life is essential, if in fact you are going to achieve them.

It's no coincidence that people who have incredible ability or who have done remarkable things are also passionate about achieving their goals. They believe in their abilities and act accordingly. This is the kind of confidence that moves you forward. Build yours to a healthy level, then tap into it often. Below are six more resources for improving your life.

Hobbies

The sixth resource for change is hobbies. They are valuable because they are often reminders of your hidden talents. They test your ability to concentrate, focus and create. With so many types of special-interest activities, the problem is how to focus on just a few. Hobbies require time to pursue. In exchange for your time, you get enjoyment.

I remember as a child loving to paint with watercolors. I had a special suitcase with leftover paints that someone had given to me. Whenever it rained, I would take out this suitcase and make use of my time indoors. As I quietly painted, I pursued something that came from the inside out. I gave myself a gift that I created.

Hobbies are a good kind of selfish activity. They often are a reflection of your dreams, desires and true affections in life. Hobbies can help you answer the question, "So, what do I want to do?" By their very nature, hobbies get you involved in activities that bring you pleasure. When you select your projects, consider the pursuit of a particular hobby.

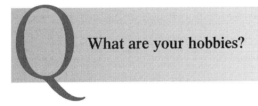

What are your hobbies?

Sense of Humor

There are many people who make their living making people laugh, yet they've never taken their own happiness seriously. But laughter is serious business. Having a sense of humor means being able to look for the unexpected in everyday occurrences. When your mind is taken off guard by the unexpected or the unpredictable, the result is laughter.

The ability to find humor in everyday life is a tool. It allows you to keep things in perspective. Without a sense of humor, situations that fall under the category of small stuff can take on a significance all their own because you can't accept the silliness of your ways.

We all make mistakes in life. But the worst mistake is failing to recognize our humanity. Laughing at the ridiculous, smiling at the imperfections of others and rolling your eyes at things you can't control are valuable resources for life.

> *If you can find humor in anything, you can survive it.*
> —Bill Cosby

Another benefit of having a sense of humor is that other people feel they are allowed the privilege of being human, too. People with whom you interact on a daily basis may be more likely to accept your desire to take risks if they know you don't criticize their own risk-taking. By responding to the people around you with a lighter, more joyous outlook, you create a different outcome than if you looked for things to be a certain way or criticized or judged. Be willing to be surprised. Remember, having a sense of humor means looking for the unexpected in everyday occurrences. So laugh.

Kaitlin's Tale

One Sunday morning as my five-year-old and I walked out of church, she looked up at me with questioning eyes. I asked, "What's on your mind, Kaitlin?"

Kaitlin answered, "Well, everyone in church was coughing today."

"They must have had colds," I said, then placed a hand on her shoulder and gently pushed her in the direction of the car.

But Kaitlin stood her ground, her feet firmly planted. She looked up at the sky. After a moment she tugged on my arm once more and asked, "Mommy, when God sneezes, do the angels say, 'You Bless You?'"

Laughter that results from having a sense of humor has emotional and physical benefits; the very act of laughing has remarkable healing effects. The body's immune system appears to be able to resist and fight off disease through a regular regimen of laughter therapy, while those who are depressed often find themselves frequently ill. The body does not separate itself from the mind. Laughter is good medicine.

> *Humor is just another defense against the universe.*
> —Mel Brooks

Another great outcome of laughter is creativity. There's a physio-logical explanation for the connection between the two. The chemicals released in the brain as a result of laughing act as euphorics. They stim-ulate the thought process. More ideas are generated, resulting in more diverse possibilities. Many creativity experts suggest that a well-placed whoopee cushion could do more for corporate America's creative genius than a thousand hours of training. This is true for you, too. Discover the unexpected. Help others to notice it. Laugh more and you'll find more ways of accomplishing your life-improvement goal.

When you enhance your sense of humor, you also give your body, mind and spirit a lift. So go ahead, surprise your brain. Use laughter to your advantage. Whether you are seeking project ideas or planning how to proceed, ask yourself if it's time to laugh.

Tack it Up

Ways to Increase Your Laughter Quotient

- Keep comic books in your desk at the office.
- Look important when you read them.
- Purchase a joke calendar. Read one a day.
- Hang around funny people. Flatter them with your laughter.
- Play practical jokes. (But learn to run fast!)
- Wear crazy underwear.
- Watch reruns of *M*A*S*H* or *The Three Stooges*.
- Watch children on a playground. Kids crack themselves up.
- Look for the humor in life.
- Get a dumb dog. You'll look smarter.
- Play hide and go seek.
- Find humor in the unexpected. Laugh at life's jokes.

Knowledge

"But I'm not qualified" are words that begin a sentence and end a dream. To take full advantage of the resource known as knowledge, you need to know what is meant by the term. Don't get trapped into thinking you aren't qualified or knowledgeable enough to pursue a particular life-improvement goal. Broaden your concept of these terms, and you end up with more resources.

Your desire to learn, your ability to access information, and your recognition of what it takes to get a job done are all significant resources. Your level of education may be an indicator of what you know, but many employers care more about your motivation to be part of a team and to advance an agenda. Think more broadly about how much you actually know. Knowledge and educational degrees aren't always compatible. A door that could have opened remains shut because you assume—incorrectly—what is meant by experience or education or knowledge.

Be willing to make a list of your skills. If you need a creative résumé to help you pursue your passions, write one that lists what life has taught you and what qualifications you feel make you valuable. If you don't feel you are qualified to do what you want to do, why should someone else think so?

Have you thought about what you really know and know about? I'm not just referring to information, but how it gets processed and what becomes of it once you get it. The following is a sample list to help you take note of the different kinds of knowledge you may possess.

Sample
My Knowledge List

I Know How To:	I Know About:
Type	Human development
Access the Internet	The process of learning
Play tennis	The Boston Celtics of the 1970s
Teach someone how to swim	Some forms of cancer treatment
Garden	Time management
Turn on my computer	Counting fat grams

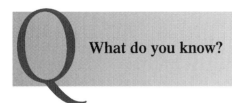

What do you know?

Life Experience

Your life has made you smarter. It has given you wisdom. As a result of everything that has happened in your life, you live where you live today. Much of this information can help you organize, remodel, renovate or rebuild your life. Not only can this awareness remind you of where it is you want to go, it can also remind you of where it is you *don't* want to go.

Taking time to reflect upon the happy times in your life, for instance, helps to clarify sources of your internal motivation. Understandably, the opposite is also true. Many of life's lessons come at a cost. Your desire to be a loving parent, for example, can come from a variety of sources. Your parents might have modeled loving parenting. But you also may have grown up not knowing how it felt to be loved or wanted. You lacked role models but, despite this, you chose to give your children what you never had. Both kinds of life experiences can be valuable sources of strength and direction. Both can assist you in your life-improvement efforts.

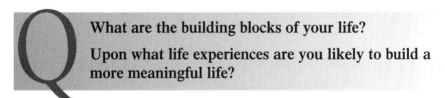

What are the building blocks of your life?

Upon what life experiences are you likely to build a more meaningful life?

Remember that there are cultural influences that have made you who you are today and can help to explain why you are you. Earlier, I shared with you a brief look at the cultural influences that shaped my decision making. When I felt free to create my destiny, I was able to let go of what was holding me in a place I didn't want to be. The important role of your cultural influences is not to hold you down, but to raise you up.

You can be shaped by events that seemed insignificant at the time, as well as by those that seemed earth-shattering. For instance, as a result how my father taught me to drive, I was given a valuable asset. Specifically, I will teach my teenage children how to drive on the oval around our local high school football field during football practice. Not only will this force them to learn how to concentrate under pressure and distraction, it will reduce their popularity enough to keep them home on weekends.

Your history shapes you for good and for bad. What you do today can be traced back to what you experienced, or failed to experience, yesterday. This is why being aware of your cultural influences combined with your life experience is a resource worth remembering.

Faith

Faith is a resource—but only if you have it. Life can often be difficult. Bad things can happen to good people. Take, for instance, the case of someone who has lost a job. Whether it was called being fired, let go, riffed, downsized or outplaced, the reality is that what once was there is now gone. Losing a job is a traumatic and devastating experience. But it's not usually something that can be controlled.

Although such an experience changes you, it doesn't have to overwhelm you. It's over. It's done. You get to decide what you do afterward. This realization can be very freeing. When you recognize that you can't control everything that happens to you in this life, the pressure to be perfect or to have the perfect life is lifted.

> *Faith keeps the person that keeps the faith.*
> —Mother Theresa

Faith is the acceptance that you can't direct the future. You can only direct what you do with what life gives you. Having a strong belief system assures you that there is a master plan. Time and again, things will happen to test your belief in this plan, but such things are actually opportunities to expand and strengthen your faith. Faith carries you when you don't think you're being carried. It gives you hope—and hope is essential to undertaking The Future Plan.

Physical Conditioning

As previously noted, your physical condition, mental state and out-look on life are all connected. Just as the hip bone is connected to the leg bone and the leg bone is connected to the ankle bone, so too are the internal components of your life attached to one another. By eating well, getting regular exercise and taking care of your body, you will have a higher energy level than if you don't do these basic "I care about me" kinds of activities. These are activities, not thoughts. Exercise is a do-it-yourself resource if there ever was one. The more you work on your body, the more valuable an asset it can become.

Achieving your life-improvement goal will take physical and mental energy. This energy needs fuel. The food that goes into your body determines how much energy will be burned, how it's burned and what you get in return. You'll think better when you eat better, you'll feel better and you'll live better. It's all connected.

> *Turns out that God is the best nutritionist of all.*
> *Take the apple. It doesn't get any better than that.*
> *Makes you wonder why people have to look*
> *elsewhere when nature provides only the best.*
> —Stacey Stimets, registered dietitian

One of the greatest benefits of taking care of your physical self is that you build up defenses to fight stress and illness. You won't get sick or run down as often, and you will be better able to move beyond those things that slow others down. Your body will be better equipped to fight off dangerous toxins. All this—just from exercising and eating right. Why ignore the connection between what you do for your body and what it can do for you? You are living in one of the most valuable resources you'll ever have—your body.

Financial Assets

The last resource listed, financial assets, is the resource most people think of first when thinking about changing their lives, and that's why I put it last. "How much will this cost?" and "Can we afford to do that?" are financial questions. Given the many other resources previously discussed, why limit your planning to strictly financial matters?

However, being practical is part of The Future Plan. At some point in selecting what life-improvement goal to pursue—or what projects will get the job done—you need to estimate your income, subtract your expenses, and make sure that what's left can meet your monthly living expenses. This needs to be done while considering the changes you desire. Because of the complexity of this process, the entire next chapter is devoted to financial management.

There is always more than one way to get the job done and still afford the work. To achieve your dream life, you have to get creative not only with your project ideas, but with how you are going to afford them. Think beyond the financial concerns for now. Think about what you have at your disposal—all twelve of your potential resources for change.

Hitting The Nail on The Head

\ You are better than you think.

\ Hobbies can hold the keys to discovering your true passions.

\ A sense of humor is often undervalued, but it is essential to forward movement.

\ Faith can carry you when all else fails.

\ Money is just one of many useful resources for achieving your life-improvement goal.

\ When someone pays you a compliment, respond with, "Thank you. You're very perceptive."

\ Life's experiences are valuable resources.

Getting What You Want on a Do-It-Yourself Budget

> *Sometimes one pays most for the things one gets for nothing.*
>
> —Albert Einstein

One of my fondest teenage memories is of my father's attempt to fix the kitchen sink. He had been asked by my mother to "take a look at the kitchen faucet." Although Saturday was his golf day, he reluctantly got out his toolbox and headed for the kitchen. His frustration grew as time passed. Then I heard a loud clank. Whatever he had been fixing apparently broke off. Next came the water.

Maybe it was the teenager in me, or maybe it was the water dripping off his nose—drip, drip, drip—that made me laugh uncontrollably. This probably wasn't smart on my part. But then I heard my father laugh. "I know better," he muttered as he picked up the phone and called a plumber. Then he grabbed his golf clubs. I was still laughing—drip, drip, drip …

People do what they can afford to do. In the last chapter, you were encouraged to look beyond money as the sole resource for enhancing your future. In this chapter, the focus is on money—how it affects which design-build project you select or which action items will get your work completed. This chapter is also about making responsible financial decisions. It looks at how to create financial opportunities and options while encouraging creativity.

How effective are you at financial management?

For instance, there are ways to accomplish the same outcome by doing it yourself. Although my father ended up hiring someone to finish the plumbing job, he did attempt to do the work himself first. He gave it a shot as a measure of his resourcefulness. On the one hand, hiring a personal trainer, nutritionist and joining a health club will cost you money; on the other hand, charting what you eat, walking a half-hour a day and drinking more water will cost you almost nothing in dollars and cents. You can pay someone, or you can do it yourself. They often get the same results.

Knowing how to manage, record, project and account for your income and outcome are significant and teachable skills. You can become more proficient, if needed, in your abilities to reduce expenditures and generate more income. This option may give you the financial freedom you need to risk enhanced happiness. Effective money management also involves seeking the proper guidance, looking for alternative means of obtaining resources and knowing how to ask the right kinds of questions.

Asking good questions is fundamental to the success of The Future Plan. The more questions you ask about how to reduce expenditures and generate more income, the more options you will create for yourself. Making lists and lists of questions about potential income sources and using the tools that will be available in this chapter may generate a variety of realistic responses. But you have to pose the right kinds of open-ended questions.

> **What have I ever made money doing in my lifetime?**
>
> **What agencies are available that could help me decide what I could do?**
>
> **What agencies are available that could find me part-time work?**
>
> **Do I have a marketable hobby?**
>
> **Who do I know who is getting paid to do something I think is fun?**

Knowing how to get cash or acquire income is another trait of financial management. You don't always need cash to accomplish your life-improvement goal, but, for higher-level projects in particular, knowing how to get cash is valuable information. The particular projects you select will determine the sources of income from which you can choose and how much income you will need. By intention, things such as start-up costs and one-time expenses have not been mentioned until now because they are project-specific. If you think money first, you limit your project ideas.

Going with Less to Get More

The ability to reduce expenditures can offset the need to generate more income—or any income. Part of being in control of your life-improvement efforts is to recognize the many ways to reduce your current living expenses and to find ways of getting things on sale. You also need to have persistence.

From experience, I have come to be a firm believer that there are exceptions to every rule. Just because one person (or agency) tells you that what you want to do will cost too much or isn't possible doesn't mean it's true. Take insurance coverage, for instance.

When I was thinking of quitting my job, one of the major factors affecting my decision was medical insurance. Needing affordable health insurance coverage is a fact of life. It's not unusual to feel trapped by this reality. I did. But I also knew that I was ignorant of how the system worked. After asking the right questions (or enough questions of enough people), I discovered that I did have options for obtaining coverage if I chose to leave my job—contrary to what I was being led to believe. The federal government (via C.O.B.R.A.) and local chambers of commerce (via group insurance plans) had increased my choices.

Consider all your options. Inquire, appeal and persist until an alternate and affordable route is discovered.

 Do you know all of your options?

When you need funds to start work on a project, consider all your choices before assuming there is only one—especially if other people need to live off this money. (You will be held accountable for your decisions, if by no one else but you.) You don't always want to tap from the same fund that pays your monthly living expenses, for example. Look for other sources to fund initial start-up costs or one-time project expenses.

Part of being fiscally responsible is considering the potential value of consulting someone who is proficient as a financial manager or advisor. Meeting with an advisor would be an example of a potential action item as part of your planning process. In almost all situations, there is no charge for your first meeting and you get to hear what services are available to you.

In addition, a good financial planner can inspire you to be fiscally responsible, assist you in determining your financial goals, show you ways of protecting your current assets, help you reduce your debt, identify potential areas of financial liabilities and work with you to ensure your financial health. Not all financial planners will make you comfortable. Find one who meets your needs. Listen to the advice, but don't take it unless you want to.

Best-Guess Budgeting

Whether you are preparing figures for your financial advisor or for your own planning, you will need accuracy in accounting. Your impressions, hunches and best guesses won't help you get where you want to go. You can't work on a need-to-know basis when it comes to budgeting and spending money. Waiting for an overdraft warning from your bank does not qualify as balancing your checkbook. (I know; I have tried this, and it falls short of being fiscally responsible.)

When you don't have a real, accurate dollar figure assigned to your financial obligations, it's almost impossible to do higher-level projects. The risk becomes too high because of all the unknowns. Again, depending upon your personal circumstances, you may be comfortable with that level of risk. But not knowing your real numbers is a clever way of masking your doubts, fears and uncertainties. (Remember the term "limiting beliefs"?)

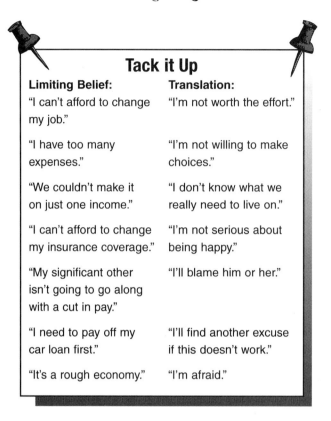

Tack it Up

Limiting Belief:	Translation:
"I can't afford to change my job."	"I'm not worth the effort."
"I have too many expenses."	"I'm not willing to make choices."
"We couldn't make it on just one income."	"I don't know what we really need to live on."
"I can't afford to change my insurance coverage."	"I'm not serious about being happy."
"My significant other isn't going to go along with a cut in pay."	"I'll blame him or her."
"I need to pay off my car loan first."	"I'll find another excuse if this doesn't work."
"It's a rough economy."	"I'm afraid."

Know your specifics. Check the actual bills that come in. Add them up. Get intimate with your finances. Replace approximations with actual dollar figures—or averages. Thinking you don't make much after subtracting child care expenses from your income is not as useful to you as knowing that you spend $250 per week on child care and earn $340 per week. Specifically, you work forty hours a week to earn $90, plus insurance. After you get over being depressed by this discovery, the information allows you to make decisions.

Part of financial management involves calculating your monthly budget. Using a fill in the blank approach, you can literally estimate your bottom line under a variety of conditions, depending upon which design-build projects you want to do. This process not only permits you to explore what you will need to spend—or do—to get the job done, but it helps you decide which projects are too expensive. Working with real numbers ensures that your decisions will be responsible, reduces your risks and permits you to pursue your dream life.

A nickel ain't worth a dime anymore.
— Yogi Berra

Acquiring Income

The list below offers creative and conventional ways of acquiring income. Whether for your monthly expenditures or for additional project costs, your project selections need to incorporate your financial situation. As mentioned in Phase Three, securing your finances will become part of your plan.

You may feel comfortable with a particular dollar figure that guarantees six months or twelve months of covered living expenses before you would ever consider quitting your job. Hence, your plan needs to include a well thought out means of acquiring six or twelve months of additional income. This could be accomplished through the sale of property, taking on another job, making a change in your investments, having an extremely large yard sale or being behind the Brinks truck when the doors fly open on the highway.

All of these actions can become projects. You may want to include them on your design-build project category lists found in Appendix C.

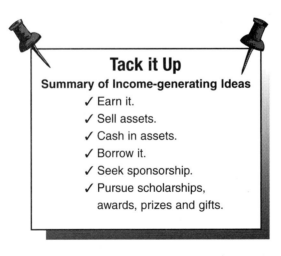

Tack it Up

Summary of Income-generating Ideas

✓ Earn it.

✓ Sell assets.

✓ Cash in assets.

✓ Borrow it.

✓ Seek sponsorship.

✓ Pursue scholarships, awards, prizes and gifts.

How much money do you think you will need, and how do you think you can get it?

Income-Generating Ideas

Your project ideas may not require additional income; if this is so, you don't have to be concerned about how to pay for your work. But if you could benefit from new income sources, take some time to sort through the possibilities. You might have additional sources to tap.

Earn it

☐ Pay yourself first (where's that coffee can?). A wonderful habit to get into is disciplining yourself to pay yourself a little extra from your budget—even if it's just a few dollars. Over time, this fund can add up and be used for the pursuit of a passion—especially if it's a low-level design-build project idea.

☐ Get a second job to supplement your income or afford your passion. But set income goals and deadlines for yourself and continue reducing expenditures, because a second job cuts into your time considerably. Try to find one related to your passion. Your goal is to be able to enhance the quality of your life, not make it worse!

☐ Is there a service or skill that you could provide on an occasional basis for which you could be paid? For instance, if you are good at wallpapering, would you be willing to let your friends know you're available for hire? If you enjoy washing windows (or even if you don't), would you be willing to offer a flat rate for washing someone's windows?

Sell assets

☐ Liquidate property by selling something you own. (Do not sell something belonging to someone else—that is bad.) When you begin truly to rank the importance of those things in life that bring you happiness, you'd be surprised at how much you can do without. Ask yourself, "What do I own that has value, but not as much to me as the pursuit of my passion?" You could have a yard sale or put a For Sale sign on that canoe that's been sitting in your garage for three years.

☐ Sell off more valuable assets, such as a new car, and replace with less expensive ones, such as a used car. Bank the difference until you have the amount you need. Ask, "What am I willing to sacrifice, exchange or give up to find true meaning in my life?" You can do with less, whether you own something or are still paying it off. If living within your means translates as not being happy, then reduce the value of what you own: your residence, automobile, food selections and so on.

Cash in assets

☐ Cash in one or more of your investments. In my opinion, it's best to consider this option in consultation with a financial advisor. There are so many tax laws that affect how much of an investment you'd actually see from early withdrawal, for instance, that you want to ensure the you come out ahead. This doesn't mean this isn't a viable option. But such transactions are closely regulated by ever-changing laws. Be sure you are up on the latest rules and regulations before you do something you can't reverse. A reliable financial advisor will provide you with the information you need to make an informed decision.

☐ Set up investments that can be cashed in. Depending upon your timeline, you could start investing now for your dream life. As part of your planning efforts, explore how much you would need over an amount of time and set your goals accordingly. Effective financial planning also allows you to consider options into retirement and alternative means of covering major expenses such as your children's education. I was shocked to learn that if I had started a steady plan of investing five years earlier than I had (which would have been at a time when I thought I could least afford it), I would literally be hundreds of thousands of dollars ahead by now.

That kind of planning (because of compounding interest and a healthy stock market) can free up other investments for pursuit of your passion.

☐ Go from owning to renting or leasing. This action may or may not represent a drastic option. You could sell your car and lease one. You could sell your house and rent. You could sell your wind surfer and rent one only when you need it. Such an option can be freeing. You can also borrow rather than buy.

Borrow it

☐ Take out a small business loan. Depending on what your project entails, loan opportunities at reasonable interest rates may be available to you. The Small Business Bureau is a good place to start, as is your local Chamber of Commerce. Inquire about your options. Visit banks. Find out what you need to prepare for such visits (a business plan and personal financial statement, for instance), and contact someone if you need help in these preparations. Then do it.

☐ Take out a home equity loan. The value that has been accumulating on your home—if applicable—is available at a set interest rate. What do you need to do to qualify? Contact your local bank or shop around. Mortgage companies also offer home equity loans.

☐ Borrow from your savings. The term "borrow" implies that something taken will be returned. Any decision to borrow from your savings—or a collective pool of savings—requires careful consideration, for obvious reasons. Again, the urgency and priority of your project comes into play in your decision-making, as does your personal situation. When you withdraw from your savings, you need to think about how much needs to be returned and on what schedule. What is a reasonable amount to borrow?

☐ One of your last resorts, in my opinion, is to borrow from someone you know. Because this is your dream life you're trying to fund, be careful not to make your problem someone else's problem—especially when it comes to borrowing money. The risk is that you may not be able to pay it back as scheduled (or even at all). Unless there is a clearly established arrangement, in writing, borrowing from people you know takes the ownership of your life and gives it to others. Only you can determine the appropriateness of making such a request.

Seek sponsorship

☐ Solicit a grant or the financial backing of a corporation that would hook into your idea. Professional athletes do this all the time. But you don't have to approach Nike. Identify potential sponsors that may be relevant to your goal. Sponsorship can take many forms. Exchanging advertising and exposure for real dollars is just one. Goods and services, rather than money, can also be exchanged.

☐ Depending upon what you want to do, some federal and state agencies give grants for start-up programs. There are also private agencies and foundations. The Internet is a wonderful source of information on available grants and funding sources. In fact, the applications for many such grants are included on various Web sites.

Pursue scholarships, awards, prizes and gifts

☐ Special occasions usually involve exchanging gifts. Instead of presents for your birthday, Mother's Day, Christmas, Valentine's Day and so on, consider establishing a Future Fund. Let others know that, as a gift, they can make a contribution to your special dream fund. Be creative, and call it whatever you'd like!

☐ The rule of any contest is that if you don't enter, you'll never win. Many towns, professional organizations, community agencies and so on run contests. Fast food chains, car dealerships, television shows and department stores run contests. Somebody has to win, so why not enter? Look through magazines and organizations that are related to your dream to see if they have any contests (or sources of scholarships) available. What can you do to help your odds? While you obviously can't bank on winning a contest, your hard work may pay off—depending upon the nature of the contest. Again, what do you have to lose?

What are you willing to do to reduce your expenditures so you can free up financial resources?

How to Reduce Your Expenditures

You don't have to generate additional income if you can absorb new expenditures by reducing existing expenditures. This is a simple concept that is often overlooked. If you want something badly enough, you'll find you can make substitutes and live without some things. This is living life according to your priorities and involves learning how to cut back.

☐ *Travel differently.* One way to do with less is not to buy a new car every couple of years and, instead, drive one that's paid off until it starts to cost you serious repair money. Another way is to go from two family cars to one. A third way—especially if you live in a city—is to sell your car outright and take public transportation! All three require a shift in attitude, a new way of coordinating efforts and a willingness to be inconvenienced in order to make the kind of life changes you want to make.

You can't spend what you don't have.

☐ *Focus.* Another area to focus on might be the weekly food bill. For example, I made a conscious effort to eliminate fast-food lunches while running errands with the kids. This resulted in a savings of almost $20 a week—or $1,040 a year! I bought large cheese pizzas at the grocery store instead of ordering out or going out for pizza weekly; instead of $15 (or more) a week, I spent $5 and saved $10 a week—or $520 a year! I cut in half my twice-daily stops at Dunkin' Donuts and went from $4 worth of coffee to $2 per day—a savings of $730 per year! If I had eliminated this practice altogether, I could have saved $1,460 a

Which expenses could you reduce which, when taken cumulatively, would significantly enhance your bottom line?

year—but let's not get carried away! These three changes in behavior resulted in a total savings of $2,290 a year.

☐ *Barter.* Find someone who can share something with you, in exchange for something you can offer in return; this can save you literally thousands of dollars. For example, if you need child care, find someone who is willing to trade off with you. If you are an accountant and need your house painted, is there a painter who could use a good accountant's services in return? Ask around, or look through the Yellow Pages. If you have a child who has clothes that would fit someone else's child, hand them down; look for someone who would be willing to give your child a few hand-me-downs in return.

If you reach out to your community, family and friends with the request to trade down, the worst that can happen is you end up giving good clothes to someone who needs them without getting anything back in return. The best thing that could happen is that you've saved hundreds of dollars on clothes for your children. Often all it takes to trade off or trade down is creative thought, a willingness to ask and some expenditure of energy—not money.

You can apply this practice to almost any expenditure— even a graduate degree. Consider becoming a teaching assistant, research assistant or living on campus in a residence hall as a residence hall director in exchange for your graduate school tuition. Often it just takes asking enough questions of enough people to find ways to eliminate or reduce expenses in exchange for what you already have—your talents, resources and time. My father used to say "you shouldn't have to pay for graduate school." He was right.

☐ *Be frugal.* It's hard to fight the powerful influence of advertising, but another way to trade down is to be much more conscious of your energy expenditures. Take gasoline, for instance. How many times a week do you drive your children to the same place where someone you know is also driving their children? Imagine how much money you could save in gasoline if you and a coworker alternated months of driving to work? A 50-percent reduction in gasoline expenses certainly adds up month after month. If there's no one in your office who wants to car pool (or with whom you want to car pool) find out if there are others in a nearby office building.

Do the Math

This chapter is about taking financial responsibility—not an easy skill for those of us who don't like to be tied down to the details. Yet this is an essential skill for change. It gives you the facts. In the back of the book, Appendix G contains a budget sheet entitled, "Life-Improvement Budget Worksheet." It's designed to help you identify all of your monthly expenditures. The goal of this worksheet is to leave you with a better bottom line.

The Life-Improvement Budget Worksheet provides a place for you to record how much money you actually spend in a month, how much you need to spend in a month, and how much is available for various projects. It allows you to calculate how much your life change will cost you in real dollars and helps you reduce costs by making adjustments to

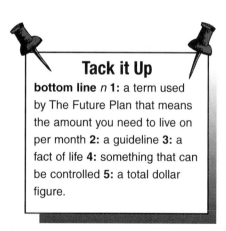

Tack it Up

bottom line *n* **1:** a term used by The Future Plan that means the amount you need to live on per month **2:** a guideline **3:** a fact of life **4:** something that can be controlled **5:** a total dollar figure.

your monthly budget. Five project columns are provided for you to record adjusted or new figures, depending upon which projects you are considering. This is an extremely effective way of determining what you can realistically afford to change in your life.

Another goal of the worksheet is to show you places where you can make adjustments. The Future Plan is based on the premise that you always have choices and that choices have consequences. If you keep running up your monthly phone bill, you will have to allow for a significant amount of money to pay for it. Your other option is to eliminate the expense by writing more letters. You can make conscious choices now that will give you freedom down the road.

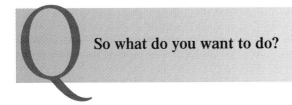

So what do you want to do?

The budget worksheet in Appendix G allows you to explore your options and project expenditures based upon a new and improved you. Make room for your projects by itemizing actual monthly expenditures in a before and after manner. Then you can allocate the resources you will need, adjust other expenses and be on your way to living your dream life.

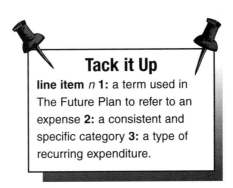

Tack it Up

line item *n* **1:** a term used in The Future Plan to refer to an expense **2:** a consistent and specific category **3:** a type of recurring expenditure.

Line items are also found on the far left column of the budget worksheet. Next to each line item is a column for you to record what you spend on each line item on a monthly basis. Line item expenses are predictable. Examples include food, travel, home or living costs, health expenses and so on. Line items are broken down even further so you can accurately calculate what contributes to your monthly expenses.

You can estimate the total line item figures for each category, or you can fill in the details and come up with an accurate line item amount. This process, although tedious at first, will be more useful in determining areas in which to make reductions or changes. If you only know the annual figure, divide that by twelve to find the monthly estimate.

The overall purpose of the budget worksheet is to assist you in being accurate in your conversations and subsequent planning. You can't do what you can't afford. That's why being open to the possibility of other ways of reducing your expenditures is an important component of The Future Plan. By redefining essentials, you are free to eliminate limiting beliefs and to live differently. To complete your budget worksheet, you may have to consult your checkbook or review your files. To be most helpful, try to avoid best guesses and use actual numbers. The more specific you are, the more realistic your bottom line will be. You might be surprised at what you discover.

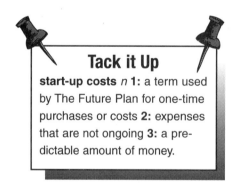

Tack it Up

start-up costs *n* **1:** a term used by The Future Plan for one-time purchases or costs **2:** expenses that are not ongoing **3:** a predictable amount of money.

The budget worksheet found in Appendix G also allows for the planning of projects that require one-time expenditures only. Start-up costs are those expenses that you incur for your project ideas that are not ongoing. If they were ongoing, you would add a line item expense on your monthly budget. Examples include initial office supplies, computer systems, essential equipment, attorney fees and the like.

The project ideas you select will influence your decision-making. However, if you can make the distinction between one-time expenses and start-up costs versus continuous monthly expenses, the process is straightforward and simple. Refer again to the punch lists you produced or will produce in Phase Four (found in Appendix D). What will cost additional money, as opposed to changing your line item expenditures? Account for these expenses only once so that your final financial projections are as accurate as possible.

What start-up expenses or one-time costs are involved in each of your project ideas?

Project Estimating

Before completing your budget worksheet, you need to consider one last factor—your income. What are your sources of revenue? Where are the finances currently covering your expenditures coming from? One of the most exciting characteristics of The Future Plan is its versatility. It can be applied to a wide variety of personal circumstances whether you are the sole provider, half of a dual-career family, single and living at home, or out on your own.

How does the source of your income influence your decision-making?

If the working half of a single-income couple wants to do a major life renovation like leaving one job for another that pays less, it stands to reason that there will have to be some adjustments made. What does this mean to the other half? Think through your ideas, talk them through and be creative.

Basic accounting suggests that when you subtract your monthly living expenses from your monthly expenditures, you want to be in the black—and, ideally, you'd like to have some money left over.

Once you've done your calculations and had some time to rework your figures, put away your calculator! You've done enough math and can move on to the next concept (and chapter). But your efforts up to this point have given you valuable information. You have a better sense of your monthly expenditures. You have a better sense of your worthy income. Both are based on your well-thought-out priorities in life. Two questions remain, however: When all is said and done, how much are you willing to sacrifice to live in your dream life? How much are you willing to spend?

"I know you think change is expensive, but not changing can bankrupt your soul."

> *It seems to me we can never give up longing and wishing while we are alive.*
>
> —George Eliot

*E*mpower You

Most people are convinced before they even start to consider making changes in their lives that they simply can't afford them. They can't live in their dream house because it's too expensive. The Future Plan doesn't empower money—and neither should you. Believe in your worth, and the financial issues can be worked out.

Empower your strengths, assets, internal resources and determination. These are the kinds of things that will buy your dream life. Money should not be the determining factor in your decision-making. As you learned in the previous two chapters, there are many resources from which to tap. Part of the fun of The Future Plan is learning how to be a walking do-it-yourself life-improvement guide—at least most of the time. (Is that a drip, drip, drip I hear?)

*H*itting The Nail on The Head

\ You can always live on less—if you value change.

\ Best-guess budgeting leads to inaccurate information and limited choices.

\ There are ways to generate income and ways to reduce your expenditures.

\ Seeking advice from others is a sign of self-confidence.

\ Effective planning often means asking effective questions.

\ Knowing your bottom line is essential to determining the level of design-build projects you can choose.

\ Reducing, eliminating or trading down are three ways to lower your monthly expenditures.

18

About Carpenter's Pencils

> *If you aren't content with what you've achieved in life, you haven't achieved it yet.*

Throughout this book you have been asked to grab a pencil to use in designing your future. But have you ever looked closely at the pencils used by contractors, carpenters and builders? They are flat, much wider than average pencils, and rectangular, not round, in cross section. Also, they don't come with erasers. Until I wrote this book, I never questioned why carpenter's pencils don't come with erasers or why they aren't round. Is it that people who use these pencils don't ever make mistakes? Or is it that they make so many mistakes they need separate erasers?

My professional builder informs me that the shape of a carpenter's pencil prevents it from rolling off roofs and uneven surfaces. Why couldn't I have figured that out? Its purpose is just to lay there. Without an eraser. Without movement.

The Future Plan, by contrast, was designed to help you move and make mistakes. Its purpose is to examine your purpose. Between all of the lines, the bottom line of The Future Plan is about achieving a meaningful life—one that is consistent with your purpose. It should be clear by now, however, that you can't spend your time according to your priorities in life until you know your priorities. It is through examination of your purpose that priorities are found. This is why this last chapter of the book returns to a fundamental question for you to ponder from this point on—let this question guide you through your life-improvement efforts.

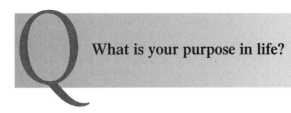

Q What is your purpose in life?

The Future Plan is how you achieve your purpose. It is a conceptual framework—you have to put on your overalls, make a pot of hot coffee and do the work. You have to decide whether to use a carpenter's pencil or that other kind. The means have been introduced, the tools provided, yet the work cannot begin until you give thought to your true purpose in life.

"So, what do you want to be *about* when you grow up?"

Once you have taken the time to determine what matters to you, the rest is a matter of planning and action. I believe you know what's important to you. The dilemma arises when you fail to believe that what matters to you is important enough to direct your life. That your purpose is worthy of pursuit. Until you come to this realization, The Future Plan or any other life-improvement effort isn't going to matter. Time will pass. Life will go by. Without rocking and without rolling.

How I Got Started

As a means of bringing together all of the concepts, phases and ideas presented in this book, I offer the most recent chapter in my life. You may discover that a completely different experience awaits you, or one that is similar to my own. Look for how The Future Plan fits into my story. This will assist you in identifying how your life will be different from now on.

The final story I share is about my own limitations and how I used what is now The Future Plan to make my life more meaningful. What happened occurred only after I accepted my purpose in life as important enough to pursue. In my eyes, I saw value in what I wanted.

Remember the little boy on the street corner during the snowstorm? He gave me permission to focus on what brought me happiness—my children. He symbolized my letting go of what I thought other people thought was legitimate, important and the right thing. I was free to answer what I discovered was a much larger question than I originally thought: "So, what do you want to do?" (which I now realize was, "What's your purpose in life?"). The answer was much simpler than I had originally thought— spend more time with my children. This became my life-improvement goal and the beginning of The Future Plan.

Feeling free to make choices, I began focusing on how I could spend more time at home with my children. Quitting my job was the most obvious choice. This decision gave me a sense of control and positive energy. The more constructive my attitude, the more productive I became. I began to think of a plan. For the first time in my married life, I took the time to assess my current situation.

Punching in the Numbers

With paper and pencil in hand and my daughter asleep on my lap, I made a list of all of the expenses associated with my working full time. I then started punching the numbers into my calculator. Lots of numbers. It was important to have an accurate account of our financial liabilities— before making any changes. So, while still employed full time, I got to work.

The first numbers that got punched into the calculator were the added expenses of child care. Then came the costs of spending quality time with my husband. Next came the added expense of hiring someone to take care of domestic chores. Finally included were the costs of a professional wardrobe, hair products, lunches, manicures, car and other "essentials" of being a full-time professional.

As my daughter remained sleeping peacefully on my lap, I hit the "total" button. I then subtracted this figure, and other set expenses, from my gross income. I remember looking first at my daughter, then at the number on the calculator, and then back at my daughter. The result was $486 in monthly take-home pay. By living everyone else's definition of having it all, I contributed less than $500 a month in additional revenue to the family.

This was useful (not to mention depressing) information. Since I had already decided to give up my job, the question changed to, "What can I do that would pay me $100 a week?" My life-improvement goal was to spend more time at home with my children, so I needed to figure out how to work from my home on a flexible schedule and net that much. During the month that followed I spent many hours talking over my ideas, concerns and thoughts with anyone who would listen—including strangers.

Where to Go from Here?

I looked into selling things from my home, considered being a day-care provider and even thought about working part-time somewhere. These represented project ideas. But since my goal was more time at home with my kids, I didn't want to put them back into full-time day-care. I was also trying to add more flexibility and freedom to my daily schedule. I kept trying to stay focused on my life-improvement goal. Simplify. Focus. Words I often spoke out loud.

Then one day in January 1993 it hit me. I wasn't sure if I knew what was involved in making a living at my new idea, but I knew where I could find out. So I got on the phone. I called everyone I could think of who had asked me to do leadership training over the past five years. I asked them if they would pay me this time and if they thought they had any need for my services in the near future. The more I spoke, the more times I used the term "professional trainer and speaker." I began hearing of other people doing the same thing. It turned out that I knew some of them. I made more phone calls. I started making punch lists.

One of the phone calls went to a man who to this day remains my mentor. We didn't know each other really well at the time, but I admired him and respected the way he conducted his life. After a few spins in my desk chair I thought to myself, "What's the worst thing he's going to say?" Not expecting actually to reach him directly, I was taken a back when he answered the phone, "Hello, friend." I then proceeded to tell him my plans. Before anyone else knew (my husband included), I told the one person I admired personally and professionally that I wanted to be like him. But the object of my admiration responded to my news with words I'll never forget, "That's nice."

What was I expecting him to say? The point of my call—in retrospect—was for confirmation, not approval. I made the call to verify in my own mind that my plan was achievable. After hanging up the phone, I began making more lists of things to do. I was well into Phase Four only months after deciding to quit my job.

By the end of the month, I had connected with three other individuals who were successfully training and speaking around the country. I was thankful and amazed at their willingness to be supportive of me in my new endeavor and their generosity in giving me hints on how to proceed.

> *People are going to pay you what you think you're worth.*
> —the Rev. Dr. Will Keim, educator, speaker and author

Changing Over

One of the other things I did was to have a conversation with my boss about my official last day. Being on good terms, she already knew I was going to resign—just not when. We set a deadline for my last day. What followed was a blur.

There was no turning back. My last day had been set for the end of February 1993. Not only was I busy wrapping things up at work, but I was busy starting things. I called back all of those colleagues that I had spoken to a couple of months earlier and asked straight out if they would hire me in the next few months. In the evenings I put together promotional materials, developed a contract, organized my home office, set up a filing system and started a wish list of desired office equipment. I didn't have any money for start-up expenses so I worked within the confines of our family budget.

In just under two months, I had lined up the next six months of work in my new career as full-time mother and part-time speaker and trainer. There was forward motion. I had built a new life and was looking forward to what each new day would bring. I was giving myself permission to be happy again. I was also thinking about how often I wanted to work and how to establish balance. My life-improvement goal was to have more time with my family—something I continue to focus on, not always as successfully as I'd like. (Guess that means I'm human.)

There were setbacks. Up to my very last day of full-time employment I was still trying to work out insurance issues. My faith in people continued to grow as professionals in human resources went out of their way to double-check a policy, look for an alternative bill-at-home plan, challenge existing regulations prohibiting a change in coverage mid-year, and make sure I was receiving continued benefits. My attitude continued to become more and more positive. "Can't do it" simply wasn't an option any longer.

When I finally dropped my keys on an empty desk, a place that had once been where I wanted to be, I paused. Something drew me back to my desk chair. As I sat and spun around as I had a hundred times before, it was different. I had made it different. This time as I spun, a distinct "Wee!" could be heard in the outer office. My children were on my lap. The oldest was twenty-two months and he made the most noise. My seven month daughter kicked her feet. When I closed the door for the last time, it ended a chapter in my life and at the same time started a new book—one that I would write. I had discovered my purpose in life and was trying to let it guide my life.

> *It isn't until you come to a spiritual understanding of who you are—not necessarily a religious feeling, but deep down, the spirit within—that you can begin to take control.*
>
> —Oprah Winfrey

Eight years later, my purpose in life is clear and I continue to look for ways to be there for my family, make a difference in other people's lives and maintain a balance that works for me. The more I learn about life, the more I realize how much I still have to learn. I'm not sure what the next chapter of my life (or book) will bring, but I do know that I'm going to have a carpenter's pencil in my hand—one that lacks an eraser and won't roll away. I have faith in that. I will get to write some of the pages.

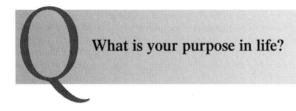

What is your purpose in life?

You too have a place to start and a life to write. The Future Plan has given you a means to make life improvements. It has given you design-build project options based on your level of comfort with change. Now it's up to you. You have a way to start creating your future. Take the time to ponder, wonder and wander. Get to know yourself even better than you think you do. For it is within you that there is an answer. When you take the time to accept your answer as worthwhile, then you have given yourself the freedom to be. You are free to live your life, not by chance but by design.

Hitting The Nail on The Head

\ Carpenter's pencils but serve a useful function.

\ The Future Plan is a set of blueprints for making life improvements.

\ Believe this: your purpose in life is worth pursuing.

\ The Future Plan originated from real life experience. It works.

\ Never spin in your office chair unless your door is closed.

\ The future is yours to create.

Appendix A

AS TIME GOES BY

Directions: In the spaces provided, list the roles you assume on a regular basis (i.e., the course of a week) and the amount of time you spend—on average—carrying out each role.

Role	Examples of Filling Role	Hrs. Per Week
TOTAL =	(Make sure total = 168 hours)	168

My Life Now as a House

Directions: Draw how your **present** life would look, as if it were a house. Remember, the size of each room needs to be directly proportional to the amount of time you spend in that particular room (or role) in the course of a week. One square equals one hour. A week totals 168 hours (24 hours x 7 days). Practice on this page: cross out lines, erase, enlarge or shrink rooms. Use the next page for your final, accurate drawing.

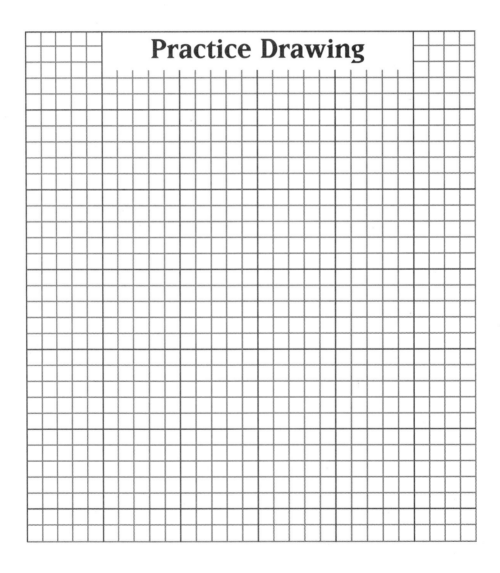

Practice Drawing

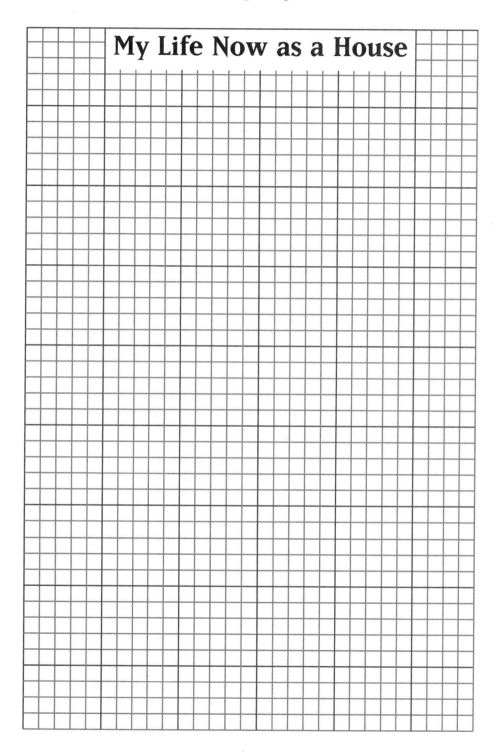

My Life Now as a House

Appendix B

My Dream Life Drawing

Directions: Draw your **dream** life as if it were your house—how you *want* your life to look. Follow the directions given in Appendix A for house size. Practice on this page. Use the next page for your final, accurate drawing.

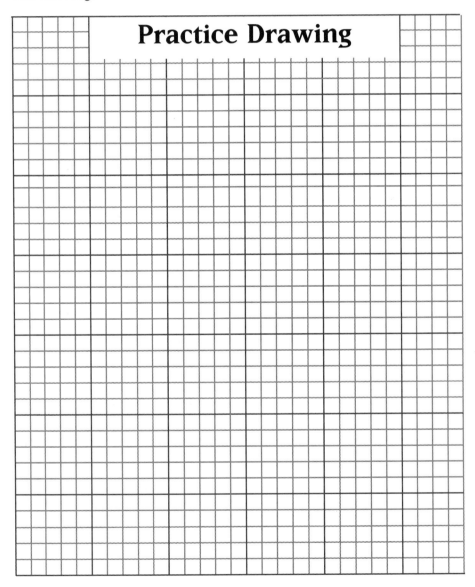

Practice Drawing

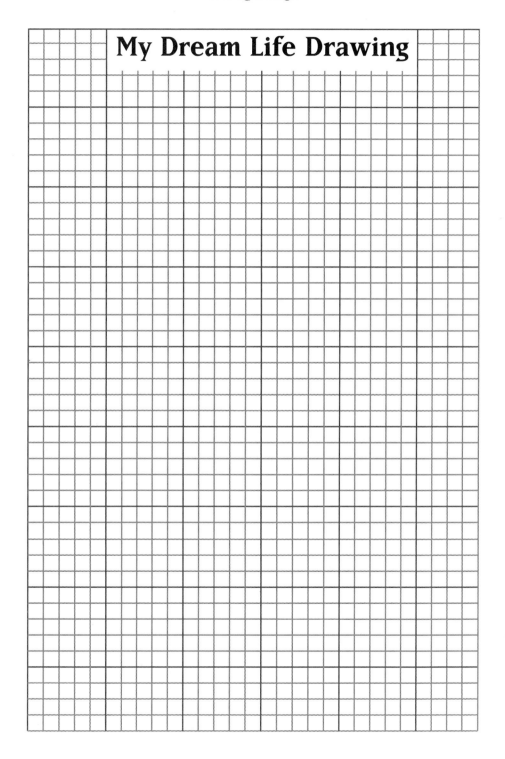

My Dream Life Drawing

Appendix C
Design-Build Project Category Charts

Four separate lists are provided on the following pages, one for each design-build project category. Pick a life-improvement goal of the highest priority from the list you generated at the end of Phase Two (found in Chapter 8)—or go with a new one. Use the **same** life-improvement goal for **each** level.

Once you have project ideas on all four charts, go back and write down any potential considerations that could affect your decision-making down the road. Ask yourself, "What do I need to think about to do this project?" and "Who do I need to help me with this project?"

As a reminder, a summary of each design-build project category is provided below. Review these as you prepare your lists. Have fun! Dream!

Level 1: Site Organization
Objectives of Site Organization Projects
- To organize your life.
- To clean up your surroundings and attitudes.
- To throw out the stuff you no longer need in your life.
- To make room for change.

Level 1 projects have to little or no involvement with others. You can take on many Level 1 projects at once. The risk is minimal.

Ask yourself questions such as, "What aspect of my life needs to be better organized?" and "What (or who) around me do I want to get rid of?" and "What is taking up space in my life that I don't need or want?"

Level 2: Remodel
Objectives of Remodeling Projects
- Adjust attitudes that lead to changes in existing structures.
- Change the way you've always done something; that is, become more efficient.
- Examine current relationships.
- Alter your level of involvement in existing organizations and relationships.

Level 2 projects have little to moderate involvement with others, but there is an impact on the lives of others based upon your work.

People begin to notice and respond. You can take on a couple of projects at this level, but not as many as with Level 1.

Ask yourself such questions as, "What do I want to be either more or less involved in, and how?" and "What aspect of my personality needs adjustment so I'll be able to achieve my dreams?" and "What can I change?"

Level 3: Renovate

Objectives of Renovation Projects
- Add related actions, attitudes and things to your life.
- Take away or add attitudes and things from your life.
- Start a significant level of involvement in external agencies.
- End a significant involvement in external agencies.

Level 3 projects require or have a moderate to high impact on others. You usually need the assistance of others to add or delete significant aspects of your life. In all cases, there is an impact on the lives of others, based upon your work. People notice and respond. You can take on a couple of projects at this level.

Ask yourself questions like, "What course could I take that is related to the pursuit of my passions?" and "What could I delete from my life that would allow me more time to pursue my passions?"

Level 4: Rebuild

Objectives of Rebuilding Projects
- Remove one aspect of your life and replace it with one closer to your passion.
- Build something new from the ground up that is more directly related to your passions.
- Consider how you'd be spending your time if this was your last year on the planet—and then do it.
- Make your life significantly different from the way it was before.

Level 4 projects require or have a high impact on others. You most likely will need the assistance of others to make the way you spend your time reflect your true passions. Keep in mind the complexity that often accompanies this level of project and the need to devote a significant amount of your time to rebuilding.

Ask yourself questions like, "What would I do for a living if I were going to die a year from today?" and "What big change in my life would make my life more meaningful?"

LEVEL 1: Site Organization

My life-improvement goal: _____

_____

My site organization project ideas:

1. _____

_____

_____

_____

2. _____

_____

_____

_____

3. _____

_____

_____

_____

4. _____

_____

_____

_____

5. _____

_____

_____

_____

6. _____

_____

_____

_____

Personal circumstances to consider:

1. _____

_____

_____

_____

2. _____

_____

_____

_____

3. _____

_____

_____

_____

4. _____

_____

_____

_____

5. _____

_____

_____

_____

6. _____

_____

_____

_____

LEVEL 2: Remodel

My life-improvement goal: _____

My site remodeling project ideas:

1. _____
   _____
   _____
   _____

2. _____
   _____
   _____
   _____

3. _____
   _____
   _____
   _____

4. _____
   _____
   _____
   _____

5. _____
   _____
   _____
   _____

6. _____
   _____
   _____
   _____

Personal circumstances to consider:

1. _____
   _____
   _____
   _____

2. _____
   _____
   _____
   _____

3. _____
   _____
   _____
   _____

4. _____
   _____
   _____
   _____

5. _____
   _____
   _____
   _____

6. _____
   _____
   _____
   _____

LEVEL 3: Renovate

My life-improvement goal: _____

_____

My renovation project ideas:

1. _____

_____

_____

_____

2. _____

_____

_____

_____

3. _____

_____

_____

_____

4. _____

_____

_____

_____

5. _____

_____

_____

_____

6. _____

_____

_____

_____

Personal circumstances to consider:

1. _____

_____

_____

_____

2. _____

_____

_____

_____

3. _____

_____

_____

_____

4. _____

_____

_____

_____

5. _____

_____

_____

_____

6. _____

_____

_____

_____

LEVEL 4: Rebuild

My life-improvement goal: _____

_____

My rebuild project ideas:

1. _____

_____

_____

_____

2. _____

_____

_____

_____

3. _____

_____

_____

_____

4. _____

_____

_____

_____

5. _____

_____

_____

_____

6. _____

_____

_____

_____

Personal circumstances to consider:

1. _____

_____

_____

_____

2. _____

_____

_____

_____

3. _____

_____

_____

_____

4. _____

_____

_____

_____

5. _____

_____

_____

_____

6. _____

_____

_____

_____

Appendix D

Punch Lists

On the following pages are "to do" punch lists. Use them to make lists of actions you need to do to accomplish your project ideas. There are many pages of punch lists provided so you can be productive. Use these pages as you would use the backs of junk mail envelopes on your kitchen table. Remember! One punch list per project idea.

There are considerations that will be raised for every project you do—questions like, "Do you need to discuss your project idea with anyone else?" and "Financially, what is your bottom line?" and "Who do you know who can open a door for you?" Turn these questions into methods for discovering the answers. Make them part of the process. Make them into action items. You can alter your punch lists whenever you need to or when you decide to change projects you want to accomplish.

Keep in mind that one project may often be enough if it comes from a higher level design-build project category. Higher level projects take many action items to accomplish each project and often more than one project is needed to achieve your life-improvement goal. Conversely, really low-level risk projects have simple components and may not require many actions to accomplish the task at hand. Go ahead! Have fun with your list making.

Punch List Tips
1. Be specific. List tasks that represent one action.
2. Accept quantity. There will be many small tasks.
3. Be realistic. Establish deadlines you can keep.
4. Be flexible. Change is allowed.
5. Work with real information. Turn questions into actions to carry out.
6. Simplify and focus.
7. Acknowledge your accomplishments with big check marks.

Punch List

Directions: Start creating your future!

Life-Improvement Goal: _____

Project Idea: _____

Priority	To Do List	Begin	End	✓
_____	_____ _____ _____	_____	_____	_____
_____	_____ _____ _____ _____	_____	_____	_____
_____	_____ _____ _____	_____	_____	_____
_____	_____ _____	_____	_____	_____
_____	_____ _____ _____	_____	_____	_____
_____	_____ _____ _____	_____	_____	_____
_____	_____ _____ _____	_____	_____	_____
_____	_____ _____ _____	_____	_____	_____
_____	_____ _____ _____	_____	_____	_____

Punch List

Directions: Start creating your future!

Life-Improvement Goal: _____

Project Idea: _____

Priority	To Do List	Begin	End	✓
_____	_____	_____	_____	_____
	_____			
	_____			
_____	_____	_____	_____	_____
	_____			
	_____			
_____	_____	_____	_____	_____
	_____			
	_____			
_____	_____	_____	_____	_____
	_____			
	_____			
_____	_____	_____	_____	_____
	_____			
	_____			
_____	_____	_____	_____	_____
	_____			
	_____			
_____	_____	_____	_____	_____
	_____			
	_____			
_____	_____	_____	_____	_____
	_____			
	_____			

Punch List

Directions: Start creating your future!

Life-Improvement Goal: _____

Project Idea: _____

Priority	To Do List	Begin	End	✓
_____	_____ _____ _____	_____	_____	_____
_____	_____ _____ _____	_____	_____	_____
_____	_____ _____ _____	_____	_____	_____
_____	_____ _____ _____	_____	_____	_____
_____	_____ _____ _____	_____	_____	_____
_____	_____ _____ _____	_____	_____	_____
_____	_____ _____ _____	_____	_____	_____

Punch List

Directions: Start creating your future!

Life-Improvement Goal: _____

Project Idea: _____

Priority	To Do List	Begin	End	✓
_____	_____	_____	_____	_____
	_____			
	_____			
_____	_____	_____	_____	_____
	_____			
	_____			
_____	_____	_____	_____	_____
	_____			
	_____			
_____	_____	_____	_____	_____
	_____			
	_____			
_____	_____	_____	_____	_____
	_____			
	_____			
_____	_____	_____	_____	_____
	_____			
	_____			
_____	_____	_____	_____	_____
	_____			
	_____			
_____	_____	_____	_____	_____
	_____			
	_____			
_____	_____	_____	_____	_____
	_____			
	_____			

Punch List

Directions: Start creating your future!

Life-Improvement Goal: _____

Project Idea: _____

Priority	To Do List	Begin	End	✓
_____	_____	_____	_____	_____
	_____			
	_____			
_____	_____	_____	_____	_____
	_____			
	_____			
_____	_____	_____	_____	_____
	_____			
	_____			
_____	_____	_____	_____	_____
	_____			
	_____			
_____	_____	_____	_____	_____
	_____			
	_____			
_____	_____	_____	_____	_____
	_____			
	_____			
_____	_____	_____	_____	_____
	_____			
	_____			
_____	_____	_____	_____	_____
	_____			
	_____			

Punch List

Directions: Start creating your future!

Life-Improvement Goal: _____

Project Idea: _____

Priority	To Do List	Begin	End	✓
_____	_____	_____	_____	_____
	_____			
	_____			
_____	_____	_____	_____	_____
	_____			
	_____			
_____	_____	_____	_____	_____
	_____			
	_____			
_____	_____	_____	_____	_____
	_____			
	_____			
_____	_____	_____	_____	_____
	_____			
	_____			
_____	_____	_____	_____	_____
	_____			
	_____			
_____	_____	_____	_____	_____
	_____			
_____	_____	_____	_____	_____
	_____			
	_____			
_____	_____	_____	_____	_____
	_____			
	_____			

Appendix E
Life Inspection Worksheet

It's time to see where your efforts have taken you in The Future Plan. Use the worksheet provided to evaluate your life as it currently exists. Skip over items that don't appear relevant now. If you only did Level 1 projects, don't pretend to have done other level projects. Be honest in your responses, and use your time as an opportunity to reflect upon your overall efforts up to this point. Return to this worksheet after you have started work on another life-improvement goal or have completed a few new projects.

Location of Property (Your Name): _____

Age of Structure: _____

    _____ **None of Your Business**
    _____ **Information Unavailable**
    _____ **Known But Not Telling**

Exterior Inspection

With regard to how your life appears from the outside, how would you describe your life?

1. Overall Condition:

    ___ Excellent   ___ Good   ___ Still Needs Work

2. Director of your life?

    ___ Me   ___ Work   ___ Significant Other   ___ Other

3. Overall Zone in which You Live:

    ___Discomfort   ___Transition

    ___Exploration   ___Contentment

4. Level of Responsibility:

    ___Overwhelming   ___Underwhelming   ___Appropriate

5. Level of Support:

   ___Nonexistent   ___Adequate   ___Increasing   ___High

6. Sense of Privacy:

   ___None   ___Plenty   ___Needs Work

7. Locus of Control:

   ___External Motivation   ___Internal Motivation

8. Appearance to Others:

   ___Excellent   ___Doing Fine   ___Faking It   ___Unknown

9. Accessibility:

   ___Handle my own problems

   ___Seek help   ___Need to Let Others In?

10. Sense of Security:

    ___Protected   ___Vulnerable   ___Uncertain   ___Increasing

11. Outlook on Life:

    ___Optimistic   ___Pessimistic   ___Improving

    ___Needs Repair

12. Sense of Community:

    ___Connected to Others   ___Lack Friendships   ___Increasing

Comments: _____

_____

_____

_____

_____

Interior Condition

1. Honest with Self:

   ___Yes   ___No   ___Needs Work

2. Honest with Others:

   ___Yes   ___No   ___Needs Work

3. Real Self:

   ___Known to You   ___Unknown to You

4. Internal Connections:

   ___Attitudes and Behaviors Match   ___Inconsistencies

5. Self-Perception:

   ___Positive   ___Negative   ___Increasing   ___Needs Work

6. Decision-Making Abilities:

   ___Weak   ___Adequate   ___Strong   ___Needs Work

7. Sense of Contentment:

   ___Weak   ___Adequate   ___Strong   ___Needs Work

8. Sense of Internal Conflict:

   ___Yes   ___No   ___Increasing   ___Decreasing

9. Self-Esteem:

   ___Healthy   ___Low   ___Increasing   ___Decreasing

10. Identity:

    ___Unknown   ___Known   ___Needs Repair

11. Self-Respect:

    ___Yes   ___No   ___Increasing   ___Needs Repair

12. Purpose in Life:

    ___Known   ___Unknown   ___Discovering

13. Roles in Life:

    ___Insignificant   ___Purposeful   ___Fulfilling   ___Not Fulfilling

14. Internal Condition:

    ___Weak   ___Strong   ___Improving   ___Needs Repair

Comments: _____

_____

_____

_____

_____

Electromechanicals

1. Physical Health:

    ___Excellent   ___Average   ___Needs Work   ___Improving

2. Spiritual Health:

    ___Excellent   ___Average   ___Needs Work   ___Improving

3. Mental Health:

    ___Excellent   ___Average   ___Needs Work   ___Improving

4. Prioritize Own Health: ___Yes   ___No

5. Stress Level:

    ___High   ___Moderate   ___Low

Comments: _____

_____

_____

_____

_____

Energy Considerations

1. Efficiency:

   ___High   ___Moderate   ___Low   ___Needs Work

2. Organizational Abilities:

   ___Yes   ___No   ___Improving

3. Power Source:

   ___Passions   ___Directed by Others   ___Money   ___Other

4. Passions:

   ___Known   ___Unknown   ___Discovering

5. Passion Pursuits:

   ___Ongoing   ___Nonexistent

   ___After Retirement   ___Improving

Comments: _____

_____

_____

_____

_____

_____

Environmental Issues

1. Personal Growth:

   ___Noticed by Others   ___Not Noticed by Others

2. Other's Responses to Your Life Changes:

   ___Positive   ___Negative   ___Nonexistent

3. Adjustment to Your Life Changes by Others:

   ___Necessary   ___Not Necessary

4. Reactions by Others to Your Life Changes:

   ___Supportive   ___Healthy   ___Sabotaged

5. Significance of Your Life Changes:

   ___None   ___Some   ___Great

Comments: _____

_____

_____

_____

_____

_____

Appendix F

Self-Assessment Inventory

SELF-ASSESSMENT INVENTORY

Directions: Place a check mark under the column that best describes how you feel about your ability to do the following list of skills on a consistent basis.

A=Always   S=Sometimes   N=Never   N/A=Doesn't Apply

		I do	this effectively	
Skill Description	**A**	**S**	**N**	**N/A**
1. Inspire others				
2. Persuade others to act				
3. Facilitate change				
4. Take initiative				
5. Write letters				
6. Speak publicly				
7. Communicate one to one				
8. Solicit feedback from others				
9. Give constructive feedback				
10. Resolve conflicts				
11. Confront others				
12. Assert myself				
13. Come up with innovative solutions				
14. Invent things				
15. Be creative and think differently				
16. Think of many ways to solve a problem or achieve a goal				
17. Manage my time				
18. Establish personal priorities				
19. Spend time according to my priorities in life				
20. Accomplish tasks in a timely fashion				
21. Anticipate a sequence of events				
22. Establish realistic timelines				
23. Avoid last-minute planning				
24. Manage my personal finances				
25. Establish a budget				

Skill Description	A	S	N	N/A
26. Be fiscally responsible				
27. Increase profit margin on sales				
28. Reduce expenditures without reducing quality				
29. Know my monthly bottom line				
30. Direct others toward a common goal				
31. Recognize the needs of others				
32. Work as a team member				
33. Encourage group participation				
34. Have manual dexterity				
35. Figure out how systems (organizations, processes) work				
36. Literally put things together or take them a part				
37. Follow directions (to build, bake, make home improvements)				
38. Create things with my hands				
39. Set up methods of efficiency				
40. Determine priorities for others				
41. Get the job done				
42. Personal maintenance (deal with relationship issues)				
43. Adapt to my surroundings				
44. Make moral and ethical decisions				
45. Lead others towards a shared goal				
46. Have a vision for the future				
47. Stand up for the rights of others				
48. Act with integrity				
Total Check Marks Per Column				

The questions above are grouped according to eight skill areas as noted in the chart below. Consider how you rated your abilities in **each** skill area. What does this tell you?

Life by Design

Skill Area	Item Numbers	What does this tell me?
Motivation	1–4	
Communication	5–12	
Creativity	13–16	
Time Management	17–23	
Financial Management	24–29	
Supervision	30–33	
Manual Dexterity	34–38	
Leadership	39–48	

Appendix G

Life-Improvement Budget Worksheet

In the columns provided, place the dollar figure that corresponds next to that line item. The remaining columns will be for you to project your monthly budgets, given specific projects you wish to pursue. Do actual expenditures first. If a particular expense item is not listed, write it next to "other" in the category that seems most appropriate. Use the spaces provided to identify the project ideas for which you are calculating your bottom line.

You may need to refer back to your punch lists for each project to estimate what is needed to finish the project. Take into account that certain line item expenses may shift, shrink, or skyrocket, depending upon what changes you are proposing to make. Also, take into account where you might be willing to reduce expenses, given the potential expense of your project idea.

My life-improvement goal: _____

_____

Project A Idea: _____

_____

Project B Idea: _____

_____

Project C Idea: _____

_____

Project D Idea: _____

_____

Project E Idea: _____

_____

AS TIME GOES BY

Directions: Under the columns marked with project letters, insert the amounts that would apply on a monthly basis for **each** project idea.

Current Expense Line Items	Current Monthly Expenses	Project Idea				
		A	B	C	D	E
Food: • snacks • take-out • groceries • household supplies • other						
Travel: • car payment(s) • car insurance • gas bill(s) • maintenance • other						

Living:
• mortgage/rent
• home insurance
• utilities
  electric
  water
  heat/oil
• telephone
• home repairs
• home improvements
• yard maintenance
• other						

Current Expense Line Items	Current Monthly Expenses	Project Idea				
		A	B	C	D	E
Health/Sundries: • insurance • out-of-pocket • prescriptions • pharmacy (aspirin, razors, soap, etc.) • dental • eyes, ears, nose • misc. (baby expenses) • other						
Clothes: • professional attire • children's • partner/spouse • recreational/casual • dry cleaning • other						
Education/ Child Care: • day care/work sitter • baby sitter (evenings, weekends) • preschool • speciality classes • supplies, books, etc. • private school/college • other						
Insurance/ Investment/Taxes: • life • disability • retirement • stocks, bonds, etc. • taxes • other						

Current Expense Line Items	Current Monthly Expenses	Project Idea				
		A	B	C	D	E
Entertainment: • family/personal • other						
Community/Church: • donations • tithes • other						
Personal Development: • day care/work sitter • health club fees • recreational activities • social groups • courses for fun • books, art supplies, etc. • skill training • other						
1. Total Monthly Living Expenses						
2. Monthly Income						
3. Bottom line (subtract line 1 from line 2)						
4. Start-up Expenses (estimated from punch lists)						
5. Adjusted bottom line (subtract line 4 from line 3)						

About the Author

Nancy Hunter Denney is a nationally known motivational speaker and leadership trainer, who specializes in organizations dedicated to making a difference in this world. She began her own company, POTENTIAL Leadership Training and Lectures, in 1993. Her intent was simple—she wanted to spend more time with her two children and continue making a contribution to others.

Since that time she has spoken to thousands of individuals, and is a frequent keynote speaker at national, regional and state conferences in higher education and other nonprofit organizations. She recently released her first video, "The Future is Yours to Create!" and a line of promotional products to reinforce her messages about life and leadership.

Nancy earned her M.A. from Bowling Green State University in Ohio, and her B.A. in Psychology and Communication Studies from the State University of New York at Oswego. Prior to becoming a speaker, Nancy worked in higher education for thirteen years.

She attends the First Congregational Church in her small New England town and is an active volunteer in her children's elementary school. She enjoys spending time with her family (and dog Jib) on their sailboat.

For more information about Nancy Hunter Denney and POTENTIAL Leadership Training and Lectures, visit www.nhdenney.com or call 1-888-566-7536.